Praise for *Home Sweet Homework*

"I've worked with Sharon for years. I'm delighted that she is sharing her wisdom with parents. It works! Her students improve their grades and find joy in life."

—Dr. Uri Treisman, executive director,
The Charles A. Dana Center,
University of Texas, Austin

"If you're a parent, you need this book. If you love a child, you need this book. If you work with children, you need this book. I can hardly wait to get this into the hands of the parents in my program. You'll want a copy; it's full of innovative and practical ideas."

—Gwendolyn Grant, president and CEO,
Urban League of Greater Kansas City

"*Home Sweet Homework* won our first ever *Author 101* Get Published, Get Publicized contest. We're huge believers! It is a comprehensive, state-of-the-art, and user-friendly guide that will help your child succeed at school. Purchase a copy today. Your children's teachers will thank you for it!"

—Robyn Freedman Spizman and Rick Frishman,
coauthors of *Author 101*

HOME SWEET HOMEWORK

A PARENT'S GUIDE TO STRESS-FREE HOMEWORK & STUDYING STRATEGIES THAT WORK

SHARON MARSHALL LOCKETT,
Founder of **Educational Innovations/SCORE**

Adams Media
Avon, Massachusetts

Published by
Adams Media, an F+W Publications Company
57 Littlefield Street, Avon, MA 02322 U.S.A.
www.adamsmedia.com

ISBN-10: 1-59869-231-3
ISBN-13: 978-1-59869-231-0

Printed in the United States of America.

J I H G F E D C B A

Library of Congress Cataloging-in-Publication Data
Lockett, Sharon Marshall.
Home sweet homework / Sharon Marshall Lockett.
p.   cm.
Includes bibliographical references.
ISBN-13: 978-1-59869-231-0 (pbk.)
ISBN-10: 1-59869-231-3 (pbk.)
1. Study skills. 2. Academic achievement. 3. Homework.
4. Home and school. I. Title.
LB1049.L63 2007
371.3'0281—dc22
2007002583

This publication is designed to provide accurate and authoritative information
with regard to the subject matter covered. It is sold with the understanding
that the publisher is not engaged in rendering legal, accounting, or other
professional advice. If legal advice or other expert assistance is required,
the services of a competent professional person should be sought.
—From a *Declaration of Principles* jointly adopted
by a Committee of the American Bar Association
and a Committee of Publishers and Associations

Many of the designations used by manufacturers and sellers to distinguish
their product are claimed as trademarks. Where those designations appear
in this book and Adams Media was aware of a trademark claim, the designations have been printed with initial capital letters.

Interior illustrations by Argosy.

This book is available at quantity discounts for bulk purchases.
For information, please call 1-800-289-0963.

Dedication

This book is lovingly dedicated to three men:

To Alton

My adopted father. Alton started my career as a teacher. Unlike the others, he never told me I "should" be a teacher. Rather, he suggested I substitute while I looked for that "perfect just-out-of-college job." He knew I'd be hooked on helping children if he could just get me in the classroom. I owe much of my life as I know it to his love, his wisdom, and his encouragement.

To Milt

My husband, my soul mate, my best friend. I was a single-again mom for over 20 years. Milt helped me to love and trust again. He taught me the wonders of new beginnings. He is my greatest cheerleader and my biggest fan.

To Jeff

My son, my joy, my source of great pride. He taught me more about teaching than I ever learned from the textbooks. He survived my many mistakes. He serves as a willing example in these pages to help you in your parenting adventures.

Contents

Contents

Contents

Contents

Foreword

More now than ever, parents are the key to the educational success of their children. Parents are their child's first teachers and lifelong advocates; parents help their children reach their life goals, even though the goals will change over the course of a lifetime. Much of my personal education career has been with university students. Parents are still the key to these students' success. There is never a time in a child's life when the support of parents isn't necessary.

All parents have great dreams for their children. Those dreams include wanting more for their child than they had themselves. Parents want their children to have the opportunity to succeed in college. It doesn't matter whether parents are grammar-school dropouts or hold doctoral degrees—they want their children to have a better life than they did.

These dreams can become reality, but to bring them about, parents must become active partners in education, from kindergarten through graduate school.

Today's classroom is not the classroom parents remember. Parents need to visit the classroom, to interact with teachers, and to become involved in all school functions to know how to integrate the new and cherish the old. Think of it as a gift you give your child: walking in to see what is being taught and how your child interacts with others. Parents need to volunteer in the classroom; schools desperately need help in the form of aides, teacher's assistants, and tutors. Serving in these positions affords you the opportunity to be first in line when your child needs help.

Preparation at home is half the battle for success in the classroom. Reading, math, spelling, communication skills . . . all these skills are really learned at home; they are demonstrated in the classroom. Home experiences are what bring about success. This book empowers parents to do a better job of equipping their children for the classroom.

The two most important subjects for your children to master are reading and mathematics. Years ago, Madeline Hunter told her student teachers, "If your children are not reading at the third-grade level by third grade, they have already failed college." Take her timely advice; if your children are not at grade level by the end of kindergarten, get help. Always be fully committed to your child's education, kindergarten through graduate school. The parents I work with commit to daily reading with their children. That simple commitment makes a dramatic difference in children's lifelong achievement.

Technology isn't an extra today; it's a standard feature. Children need to work on computers at home as well as at school. If you can't afford your own computer, you need to schedule time daily at your local library where computer access is free. A child deficient in technological skills will be at a serious disadvantage in school.

Children need to experience the classics. *The Nutcracker*, *Heidi*, *Cinderella* . . . these and other classics broaden children's dreams by showing them inspiring examples of musical, artistic, and literary creativity. Children also need to participate in sports or other group activities. These experiences teach them about both cooperation and competition in life. Your children have unique talents. It is up to parents to help children identify their gifts. Nurture their talents!

We need to make children aware of the many opportunities set before them. Ask poor students who want to go into medicine what they want to be, and they say, "I want to be a doctor." Ask a wealthy student the same question, and she may say, "I want to be a pediatric ophthalmologist." Help your children learn the nuances of the professions related to their interests; help them become as sophisticated as their wealthy friends. Enjoy helping your child explore the many opportunities the world provides.

We often grieve the fact that the "Mom, milk, and cookies" of yesteryear are gone forever. They really aren't; they have just changed. Anything you do as a family can be a bonding experience. This includes homework. Your involvement with your children in their homework is important. It sends the message that you, too, are willing to pay a price—in time and effort—to help your child be successful.

All children need someone to affirm them. They readily know their weaknesses; they need you to point out their strengths. Become their greatest fan.

I have spent a lifetime helping children develop. They are our future, and I'm optimistic. We want our children educated; we want them to have every opportunity; we want them to pursue the highest educational degrees that are available to them; we want them to do a better job of leading the world than we have.

As parents, sometimes we don't know the answers. I've had the privilege of working with parents and schools that Sharon has trained. I know that her methods work. I challenge you to put these principles into practice. You want your children to lead the next century. They can do it with the skills taught here. The parents in my program always ask for more. I can hardly wait to hand them a copy of this book!

—Kogee Thomas, Ph.D.
Former Director of Special Programs at the Center for Educational Partnerships, University of California–Irvine

Acknowledgments

Saying a mere "Thank you" to those whose foresight made this book possible is so inadequate. You are, indeed, the wind beneath my wings.

Rick Frishman and Robin Spitzman of *Author 101*, Gary Krebs and Paula Munier of Adams Media: Thank you for your vision and insight as sponsors of the *Author 101* contest. I'm ecstatic that I won. I am also grateful to you for your willingness to mentor those of us with a message and passion.

Thank you to the rest of the great staff at Adams Media for their insight, professionalism, and expertise: Gene Molter, Beth Gissinger, Brendan O'Neill, Katrina Schroeder, and Suzanne Goraj. Although your editing skills were precise, the execution was kind.

A special thank you to my staff, Linda Johns, Glen Johns, Scott Hendrickson, Laurie Rose, Michael Anguiano, Mark Hendrickson, and Darin Miller, for taking over my other responsibilities so I could meet the writing deadlines.

Thank you to those outside Adams Media whose editing expertise enriched this book: Velda Rose, and Kristi Anguiano. An extra special thanks to Joanne Simpson who donned her English teacher's red pen, kept me awake the long hours it took to meet the deadlines, and reminded me to laugh.

Introduction

Tag! You're It!

My son had been in kindergarten for five weeks. Already I had been invited by his teacher to participate in four parent conferences, one to discuss the fact that he forged my signature on his homework assignment. In neatly printed capital letters, he wrote:

JEFF'S MOM

I like parent conferences a lot better when I'm the teacher!

En route to a meeting on a college campus, a computer-made banner caught my eye. It was prominently displayed on the door of a professor of religion:

This life is a test.
It is only a test.
If it had been real,
We would have been given
Better directions.
SOURCE UNKNOWN

I have quoted it often, but nowhere is this saying more potent than when it relates to us as parents. We have a tough job, and no one can do it for us. But then, we wouldn't want them to. It is a labor of love. The Boys Town motto, adopted by Father Flanagan in 1917, says it well: "He ain't heavy. He's my brother." As frustrated and insecure as we parents sometimes are, our children "ain't heavy" either!

As parents, we never quite know:

- When we are holding on too tight and when we are letting go too soon
- When we must be tough and when we need to be tender
- When we should punish and when we should ignore misbehavior

And nowhere is our dilemma more evident than as it relates to our children in the process of learning. We struggle with such issues as:

- When to affirm their attempts at creativity and when to demand that they improve the quality of their work
- When talking to their teacher is necessary and when it would be an invasion of our children's privacy
- Whether they are being honest about their efforts in spite of poor performance or whether they have learned how to manipulate us in order to postpone a well-deserved punishment
- Why they seem to understand the material but perform poorly on their tests
- How to help them in the process of learning without assuming a responsibility that rightfully belongs to them
- How to deal with a child who learns easily but must be prodded, while another sibling struggles to perform and needs encouragement

Fortunately, there is well-researched guidance to help resolve many of our schooling questions. The goal of this book is to offer guidelines that will empower you—today's parents—as you assist in your child's education. The guidelines are negotiable in every situation and with every child—there are no rigid rules or magic answers. But there are learning principles and strategies that can be used by every parent. I intend for this book to provide sound learning strategies, illustrated with easy-to-use everyday examples and with alternative approaches to facilitate learning. In workshops, I equip teachers with a bag of tricks. When one strategy fails, they pull out another. You can learn these strategies to help your children.

Our children inherited a very different world from the one we grew up in—a world of unprecedented opportunities mingled with overwhelming problems. We have lightning-paced technological breakthroughs; nearly unlimited information available to everyone; many more mobile and single-parent families; escalating incidences of teen pregnancy, abortion, and substance abuse; wealth alongside poverty; violence alongside benevolence; and worldwide communication that is as effortless as local. Many of our children are more computer literate than we will ever be. They have information at their fingertips that we had to search for; they have ready answers to questions we didn't even know to ask. The process of learning is different for them than it was for us.

Although church and state remain mutually exclusive in this country, education and values cannot be separated. According to the National Center for Education Statistics, one in every ten twenty-four-year-old Americans (and one in every four Hispanic-Americans) has not earned a high school diploma. Our schools teach children who come from a variety of cultural backgrounds. In some schools, students speak 100 or more different language dialects. We live in a mobile society; high turnover rates result in a lack of continuity in the school curriculum. We parents *must* learn to partner with our schools. Our children's futures demand it.

Every educational reform document pleads: "We need the support of parents and the support of the community in order to accomplish the monumental task of education with today's diverse society."

Parents respond: "We're in! We are our children's first and most influential teachers. We are our children's most avid supporters. We care far more than words can say. But we don't know how!"

Arm yourselves with factual information and proven strategies. Help your children learn. Share what you have learned with teachers. You'll likely hear comments like my friend heard:

"My son was having trouble in school so I asked his teacher if she had tried a certain technique you suggested. I kept making suggestions. Finally she said, 'You know more about teaching than I do!' I suggested she attend your SCORE workshop."

I founded SCORE: Success in the CORE for Everyone! SCORE's success rate resulted in validation by the United States Department of Education in 1994. SCORE assists educators in improving academic performance by teaching study skills and providing an array of support services (*www.score-ed.com*).

Home, Sweet Homework! is organized into three sections:

Section I responds to typical dilemmas parents face relating to homework, such as whether or not our children should study with friends, finding the best way to help different types of learners, and how to deal with too much homework and too little time.

Section II provides strategies for typical homework situations, such as how to drill for a spelling test, how to memorize, and how to improve comprehension.

Section III shares strategies for dealing with your children's learning frustrations, such as studying for but failing a test.

Let me encourage you! My son Jeff and I both survived kindergarten. Today he holds a bachelor's degree and is a case manager for the Regional Center, an organization that provides services to people with developmental disabilities. In his position, he serves as an advocate for the handicapped and their families as they deal with their life and educational challenges.

If you are frustrated, as I was, hold on. The verdict won't be in for your children for years!

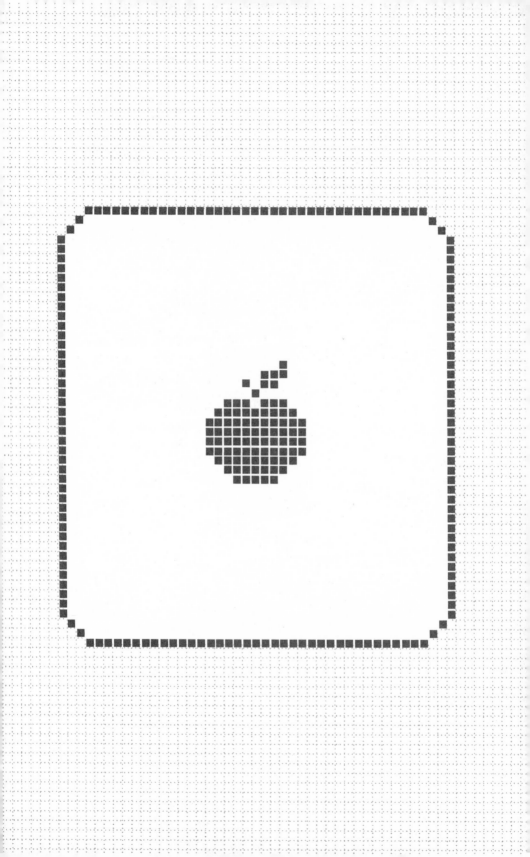

SECTION I

QUESTIONS PARENTS ASK

When I started SCORE, we admitted any warm-bodied ninth grader who would agree to spend a week in a summer live-in program at the University of California–Irvine. Joe was one of the warm bodies. Shortly after the school year began, my tutors suggested, "We need to drop Joe from the SCORE program. He's not college material."

"Why is Joe not college material?" I queried.

"Joe failed four of his five classes last year. He got a D in the other one."

Even to my Pollyanna ear, that didn't sound like college material, but every time I closed my eyes, I saw Joe's smile and his bright eyes that I had come to love during our week together. "I just don't feel good about dropping him," I replied. "Give me a while to think about it."

I looked up our summer records. This same Joe, in just one week with us, had achieved a 236 percent gain on our local exams. That was college material.

Your Child Can Learn

Barring a disability that can be medically diagnosed (and that often has been noticed before formal schooling begins), all students can perform academically through and beyond high school graduation at a quality of learning we consider to be "grade level" and "college preparatory." If you have a child who is not achieving in the classroom, there is a reason. The reasons are myriad. Lack of ability is not one of them. Neither is lack of caring. All children want to succeed.

Our brain is a marvelous machine, capable of greatness. As we learn about brain function, we are finding that the computer we wear on our shoulders is far more powerful than any machine we can create. It affects—and is affected by—everything we say, think, eat, and do. It has amazing potential.

Learning to speak is one of the most difficult academic accomplishments of our primary educational career. If your child speaks well but struggles learning to read, there may be a problem that is yet to be discovered. Barring a recognizable disorder, any child who can speak has the intelligence to learn to read, write, and calculate at the level of competency needed to gain admission to college. Since you've already taught your child to speak, you also have everything it takes to be a teacher—minus, perhaps, a few strategies and a little information.

Why, Then, Do Children Struggle to Learn?

If it is true that everyone can learn, why do so many children struggle? There are many possible reasons why a child performs poorly:

- Lack of study time by the student
- Improper study strategies by the student
- A mismatch between teaching style and learning style
- A mismatch between the way the teacher teaches and the way the students are tested
- Test anxiety on the part of the student
- Emotional problems in the student's life (if not dealt with, life issues have a "sleeper" effect. Students may continue to function after a death in the family, for example, but experience problems five or ten years later)
- Chemical dependencies (legal prescriptions, illegal drugs, steroids)
- Physical problems (such as poor eye-hand coordination, vision disorders, hearing problems, allergies, or special dietary needs)
- Reaction to prescription drugs
- Nutritional deficiencies

Helping these children is what this book is all about. Obviously, the cure is related to the cause. If your child is not performing at grade level, search for the reason and help him resolve it. Never wonder if it is lack of intelligence. Never wonder if she "just don't care." As researchers Caine and Caine state, "the search for meaning is innate." All children can learn.

I trained college and university students to work with high-school students in SCORE. I personally worked with those students they couldn't reach. I had inherited Joe.

"Tell me a little about you," I requested. "What do you want to do?"

Without hesitation, this bright (but severely underachieving) young man said, "I want to be a teacher."

I was genuinely surprised. Somehow four Fs and one D as a freshman legacy didn't add up to being a teacher. But by this time in my career, I knew how to counsel (or perhaps, more honestly, how *not* to counsel) underachievers. Rather than pointing out his failure, I began asking him about his favorite teachers, his favorite subjects, and his favorite ages, and whether he had experience working with children. A counselor friend of mine calls this process "petting your dream." Actually, we explored our common dream together—I, too, love teaching!

Soon it was time to refocus from tomorrow to today. "What are your plans for this year, Joe?"

To my great chagrin, after our wonderful time of dreaming together, Joe responded, "I think I'm going to drop out of school. It just isn't working for me."

"You could do that, but you just told me you want to be a teacher. Do you?"

"Yeah!"

"Joe, teachers have to go through college. Do you want to be a teacher badly enough to get through college?"

"Yeah!"

When you hold a child's dream in your hands, that child has chosen to make himself vulnerable to you. You have the power to help achieve those dreams; you have the power to destroy both the child and the dream. Joe and I became partners in reaching his dream.

 When you hold a child's dream in your hands, that child has chosen to make himself vulnerable to you. You have the power to help achieve those dreams.

By the way, Joe earned a 1.8 GPA and passed all his classes his sophomore year. He graduated with his class. He entered community college en route to becoming a teacher.

1

How Can I Help if
I Don't Understand It?

"I was never a good student, and learning has changed since I was in school. I'm actually a bit intimidated when I try to help. I'm afraid I'll teach him something that doesn't match what the teacher says. I'm also afraid he'll know more than I do. Isn't it enough that I love and support him without needing to help?"

Your love is always needed, but in today's world most children also need your help. And you can help even if you don't understand, even if you feel insecure, and even when your children know more about a subject than you do.

Susan, a young, married, stay-at-home mom, was illiterate. She could speak well, but she had very poor reading and writing skills. Once her first child started school, Susan would have to write notes to the teacher when her child had been ill or for other reasons. When her daughter entered first grade, the teacher invited Susan to help in the classroom. Susan, of course, was happy to be a part of her daughter's life. As she aided in the classroom, Susan learned to read and write. Looking back, she realizes that her daughter's teacher had read the poorly written notes and recognized a parent who needed help.

Susan continued to learn alongside her daughter and, later, with her other children. With the confidence she gained from learning to read and write, she took a college class, then took another. Today, she holds a master's degree and is a special education teacher.

How do *you* learn something new? When I was learning to use the draw function on a computer, I labored for hours (really!) trying to draw a box around text. I would draw the box to emphasize a section. Then I would edit the text, and everything except the box would move. I labored, printed, edited, printed, tried, asked questions, printed, and finally, I got the box just where I wanted it. I grabbed the page from the printer and ran down the row of secretaries waving my page in the air saying, "I drew a box! I drew a box!" The secretaries looked, acted impressed, applauded me, and told me what a good job I had done.

When I returned to my office, I began thinking about how silly I was running down the aisle showing my box to those who had been drawing boxes on computers for years. But their approval sure felt good!

Far more than help with content, your children need your approval. They need you to look at their honest efforts, clap for them, and tell them they did a good job.

When they were little and tried to walk but fell down, you encouraged them. You said, "You can do it! Try again. I'll catch you if you fall." You didn't say, "You must not have been concentrating while you walked or you wouldn't have fallen."

When they were little and made their first efforts to speak, you heard their strange little words and said, "Oh, she said 'daddy,' she said 'daddy'! Say it again: DAD-DY!"

 Far more than help with content, your children need your approval.

Don't change that when they get into the classroom. They need to have you tell them how smart they are. They need to hear you applaud their efforts. They need to hear your approval and encouragement. They need to know they are loved. Your encouragement and approval are far more important in their personal development and attainment than anything else you can do to help them achieve. Your number-one job is to be their most devoted cheerleader.

 They need to hear you applaud their efforts.

What to Do When You Don't Know How

When I train new tutors, I start by asking what they are afraid of as they begin this task. Always, their number one fear is: "What if I don't know the answer?"

We role-play each of their fears as part of the training. In one group, the tutor playing the role of "not knowing how to do the work" actually turned his back on the student he was supposed to be tutoring. As we discussed the dynamics of the role-play, the person playing the student said, "I thought he didn't like me."

Face Your Fear

Much of our inability to help our children stems from our personal fears; but when we allow our fear to control us, we send terrible messages to our children. In the above situation, the tutor was inadvertently saying, "You are not worth my time."

You can help your children even if you weren't a good student and even in subjects you don't understand. In fact, you will probably do a better job if you had to struggle to learn something; that struggle will help you relate to what your children are feeling.

Even those with a formal education suffer from feelings of inadequacy. The world is changing so rapidly that our children eventually reach a point where they have passed us in some areas. When my son left for college, I had to call him in the dorm when we switched to daylight-saving time. I didn't know how to reset the clocks on the microwave, computer, answering machine, or video player.

So jump in. You're it! Admit to them that you feel inadequate, but tell them you'll "give it the old college try." In doing so, you model a great life skill: taking a risk and facing your fears.

Reverse Roles

How can we help? Reverse roles. Have your children teach you! Remember that we learn far more by teaching another person than we do by having them tell us something.

If you do not speak the language in which your children are taught, you may feel extremely inadequate. But you, too, can help. Your children can translate what they are learning into your language, explain it to you, and translate it back. They will have had three exposures to the material that way; they will be three times as likely to know it. Encourage them to practice speaking their lesson to a friend in English; that gives them the benefit of a rehearsal.

I suggest this technique even when you *do* understand the content. The teacher always learns more than the students, so turn your children into teachers!

Use the Book

When I interviewed students for the SCORE program who were struggling to learn, I would say, "Let's read the question in the back of the book and then skim the material to find out what you need to read in depth to answer the question."

The students thought it was cheating to read the question first. Actually, it's a great study strategy; it alerts you to watch for key concepts as you read. My students approached all the reading tasks the same way, word for word for word. They didn't know how to skim a text to find an answer. Take advantage of what the textbook has to offer you. As parents, you can:

- Use the index to find the main ideas.
- Look at the headers within the chapters and ask your children to explain those to you.
- Look at the pictures and read the captions.

- Read the questions at the end of the book and ask your children for the answers.

If your children don't know the answer, help them skim for a key word to help them discover what to read in order to find the answer.

Have Them Restate What They Learn

When people tap into our feelings of inadequacy, our reaction is usually anger. If you notice your children are angry and frustrated with homework, it may be that they are struggling to comprehend. Comprehension is always slow when terminology and vocabulary are unfamiliar. You may observe this frustration when your children are studying subjects with a unique vocabulary such as science, a foreign language, or poetry. It also occurs often with English learners. They hear in a language they don't fully understand. They must translate it into their native language for comprehension, and then they must figure out how to translate it back into English for class discussions or testing.

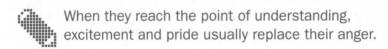 When they reach the point of understanding, excitement and pride usually replace their anger.

When you notice that your children are angry or frustrated, help them translate what they've learned into words or pictures you can understand. When they do this, they will go over the material three different times. They will hear or read it, they will convert it into a form that is common to you both, and then they will convert it back into the language of the classroom. The process will increase their comprehension.

When they reach the point of understanding, excitement and pride usually replace their anger.

Make Learning a Social Experience

I was speaking with a friend the other day who said, "I got so frustrated with this homework business. I just said to my son, 'Go to your room, and close your door, and stay there for an hour and do your homework.'"

My friend speaks for many of us. Getting homework done can be frustrating, even if we know how to help. However, when we realize that learning can be a social experience, we have a built-in set of allies. Open up your dining room table and invite their friends over. Have them sit around the table; if they're hungry (they're always hungry), provide a nutritious snack; have them do their homework together, study together, answer one another's questions, and coach one another. It's okay if they digress every once in a while. Socializing while they do homework sends an important message: "We all study."

Use friends as an asset. You don't have to know the answer; you just have to provide the food.

Call the Experts

Collect Web addresses and phone numbers of those who can help your children when you can't. Some schools have manned Web sites; some pay teachers to sit by a phone to tutor. Make sure your children have a phone number for at least one person in every class. That way, they can make a phone call when they get stuck, when they have been absent, or when they are ill.

How to Help

As you work with your children, remember that each child is unique. The technique that works with one child may be ineffective with another. The strategy that is effective one evening may be discarded by your child the next. Try one tactic; then try another.

The following guidelines will help:

Allow "Think Time"

As long as you are talking, your children are not absorbing and internalizing what they have learned. Give them time to try one approach before you offer a suggestion. That way, they "bring some thinking" to the table and are more receptive to another approach.

Let Your Child Do the Work

Rather than saying "You need a comma here," say *"You left out a punctuation mark between here and here; can you find it?"*

Rather than saying "The author was trying to say . . ." say *"What do you think the author meant when he said . . . ?"*

Rather than saying "I'll look up the answer in your text-book," say *"Where do you think you would find the answer in your textbook?"*

Rather than saying "I'll make flash cards for you," say *"This is how you make yourself a set of flash cards."*

Name It

Make sure your children understand what they need to accomplish. Some children are able to verbalize their goal; others respond better if they work from a list. Without them knowing the goal, they can dawdle and become confused.

Be Flexible

There is usually more than one way to do things. Students don't have to do their work the exact way you would. If you study more effectively with background music, they don't have to—they might need total silence. If you memorized verb conjugation using flash cards, share that with them—but don't insist that they use the same method if it proves unnatural or ineffective to them. Create options for them, and let them decide which option they find most effective. Share with them how you learn, then allow them to explore and personalize their own style.

Be Patient

Students don't have to do things right the first time they try. Give them the time, encouragement, and feedback they need in order to try again, to do a better job the next time.

Praise Their Baby Steps

In his book *Hide and Seek*, psychologist James Dobson discusses ways to build self-esteem in children. One common mistake parents make with children is to attack the child rather than the problem. See that you discuss errors and how to correct them, rather than berating, in words or attitude, the child who made the errors. In helping with homework, the message that berates the child can be subtle: "You got that one wrong again," implies the child is not smart enough to find the right answer. A more playful approach: "Oops! Seems I've seen that error before! Naughty error! How can we get rid of you?" adds a touch of humor and implies that you want to partner with your child to eradicate the problem.

Have Them Teach You

When your children are struggling, have them teach you what they have done. Rather than saying "This one is wrong," when you find an error, say *"Walk me through this one. What did you do first?"*

 We tend to remember
10% of what we READ
20% of what we HEAR
30% of what we SEE
50% of what we SEE and HEAR
70% of what we DISCUSS with others
80% of what we EXPERIENCE personally
95% of what we TEACH to someone else
—From William Glasser's *Schools Without Failure*

· · · · · · · · · · · · · · REFLECTION · · · · · · · · · · · · · ·

For some reason, Jeff's math homework was very inconsistent. He would do one problem right, but miss another that required the same skills and was about the same level of difficulty. Each evening I would check his work, mark those that were wrong, and have him correct them. Nothing seemed to change. I thought he was just being careless.

Finally, I changed my approach. I would have him go over his work, one step at a time, teaching me. When he made an error, he caught it—usually not very happily. When he made an error, our nightly homework check sounded like this:

$$
\begin{array}{r}
631 \\
\times\ 64 \\
\hline
2524 \\
37660 \\
\hline
40184
\end{array}
$$

"Four times one is four.

"Four times three is twelve. Put down the two; carry the one.

"Four times six is twenty-four plus one is twenty-five.

"Put a zero placeholder in.

"Six times one is six.

"Six times three is . . .

"Six times three is . . .

"Six times three is . . . "

He would sigh deeply and say,
"Okay. Six times three is eighteen."

With that, he would sigh again, erase the wrong number, and correct his own error. Years later, we discovered that Jeff has a vision disorder that intensifies with stress and fatigue. When he did homework late in the evening, what looked to me like careless errors actually were his eyes malfunctioning. Turning him into the teacher slowed him down enough to focus his eyes so he could catch his own errors. It also gave him some extra practice in his math facts.

 What looked to me like careless errors actually were his eyes malfunctioning.

2

How Can He Learn with the Radio Blaring?

"He drives me crazy! I nag at him to do his homework; then I walk into his room, and the radio is blaring and he has the television on. When I tell him to turn them both off, he tells me he can't concentrate without noise. It seems to be a losing battle. I certainly couldn't learn in that environment. Could he? What do I do?"

In almost every workshop, I hear this question. My response may surprise you.

One of life's great surprises is discovering that two children created by the same parents can be so different! In the same family, one child sleeps through anything while another awakens when we whisper in the room; one spits out food while another cries when we don't shovel it in fast enough. We are born with different acuities in hearing and responses to stimuli.

The Silence Myth

Most researchers will tell you that silence is necessary before learning can even occur. Most researchers are people who need quiet in order to learn. They usually find data that validates their preferences—not because the research is invalid, but because there are plenty of people who need silence. We tend to interpret data according to our prior knowledge base, and we tend to look for data that validates that with which we are most familiar.

I estimate that roughly 30 percent of our children *need* silence in order to learn; 40 percent are equally comfortable with quiet or noise. It isn't hard, then, to find data to validate the silence claim. There are people, however, for whom silence is the loudest noise—perhaps as many as 30 percent of the population. To these people, silence is every bit as distracting as noise is to those who need quiet.

Vanessa, a teacher in one of my workshops, asked if today's society creates people who thrive on chaos. If so, should we help them relax and become better adjusted by teaching them to work in silence? Yes, I think we can (and should) develop our capacities, but we usually do that by learning to compensate to meet our needs in alien environments rather than by changing our preferences. For example, a wiggly child is more likely to learn note-taking skills that allow him to move around than he is to sit still. A child who learns best to music is more likely to compose a song in her mind related to the topic than she is to block out the music. An artistic child is more likely to use note-taking strategies that require drawing than he is to block out the visual images in his mind while he listens to a lecture.

The Art of Negotiation

Now, as to the chaos in your child's study environment: attack it in stages. First have her turn off the television to avoid visual distractions. Then switch to music without words. Next, lower the volume on the radio, a little at a time so the contrast isn't too great (and so she will cooperate). Usually she is so grateful to get music that she will willingly comply. When the music is soft in the background, switch types of music, asking her to experiment with easy-listening, jazz, and classical. Most children are surprised to find that they like jazz and classical music. Most are pleasantly surprised to discover that they recognize several classical tunes; many cartoons are set to classical music. Most, after some maturing, also admit that they study better with softer and gentler music.

The Research on Music

The original research that was conducted on background music for studying concluded that classical music from the Baroque period in 4/4 time stimulates beta waves in the brain, thereby enhancing learning (aren't you glad you asked!). A more recent study called *The Mozart Effect*, from Frances Rauscher of the University of California–Irvine, validates that kinesthetic intelligence is enhanced with music. There have been several studies over the years at various grade levels, including those done by Millicent Hume Brandt, Raymond E. Mann, and Laurence O'Donnell, that indicate music, rhythm, singing, movement, and dance increase pre-reading skills and reading comprehension, and improve behavior. Entire Web sites are devoted to the benefits of music and learning, such as *www.parenting-baby. com/Parenting-Baby-Music-Research*.

You see, there are noise-needers, too. When researchers look for data to validate the noise claims, subjects are easy to find! Our children who need background music to learn know they are bothered when it is too quiet. They usually need our help to find the kind of music that will stimulate their brain in a positive way rather than the noise that detracts from serenity and learning.

The Truth Beyond the Music

Look at your children with earphones in their ears when they are studying, those who seem to be listening to music in order to focus. They may need noise in order to learn, or they may be intuitively compensating for something else that is detracting from their studies.

Observe the rest of their body language:

- Is sitting still difficult for them? They may be kinesthetic learners; they will need to act out, dance out, or quietly mouth the information they are trying to learn. Music is actually their tool for movement.
- Do they often say "I thought I had the right answer, and then the teacher read it out loud, and I thought, ooh, I missed that"? Perhaps they are kinesthetic learners; music, movement, and talking help them focus.
- How do they function in the morning or the afternoon? Some children perform better at different times of the day, for a variety of reasons. Music may be how they intuitively compensate for those times when they are sleepy or can't concentrate. They may turn on music and sing or sway to it to keep from falling asleep; they may listen to music to keep their thoughts from distracting them.
- Do they work better in bright or dim light? Some children need high levels of light; some children study better in soft light; some get headaches from artificial light. When their eyes are malfunctioning, they may know something is wrong but not be aware of what it is. They may don earplugs and music to try to block out their visual discomfort. You can't do anything about the light in their classrooms, but you can control it at home.
- Do they get restless and start making careless mistakes after studying a certain length of time? Some children need to walk outside for a few minutes in between their assignments to be able to refresh themselves. Behavioral optometrists teach children with certain visual disorders to rest their eyes this way for two minutes after every fifteen minutes of concentrated study. In the classroom, walking around is often disruptive; but they still need to break the strain on their eyes. They can simply look out the window or from their desk to the chalkboard for a few minutes. They need to break their vision from near to far in order to reduce the strain on their eyes.

The Life Tool: Theater of the Mind

Studying at home is one thing. Noise in the classroom is another. Since most tests are given in silence, students who need sound must learn how to create sound so they can focus in silent rooms without disturbing others. They can create noise silently through the "theatre of the mind." Before beginning the test, they close their eyes and begin hearing the beat to a favorite song. About four measures into the song, they open their eyes and start the test, continuing the beat in their minds. They take their test to music that they alone can hear by using the theater of their mind.

Many children who need noise also learn best by listening, moving, and talking. During tests, they are helped by silently mouthing the words or by swaying quietly at their desks to a rhythm that only they can hear. They can get their auditory stimuli with no sound at all!

·················· **REFLECTION** ··················

During an in-service, I mentioned that some people need noise. A participant commented emphatically, "I can't believe that my silence bothers them nearly as much as their noise bothers me!"

I asked the "noise-needers" in my audience to help her understand. They told stories of visiting the country and having to turn on a fan before they could sleep because they could not shut off their thoughts without the sound of traffic noise outside. They told of nervous behavior during tests such as fidgeting and clearing their throats. As children, they were unaware that these behaviors were an effort to fill the void created by too much quiet. Finally, the woman commented, "Well, I guess I have to believe you, because you're teachers like me, but I will never understand it."

You may never understand it either, but teach your children who need noise to compensate in order to master the classroom.

3

To Friend or Not to Friend?

"I'm so sick of the homework issue! I try to help, but she sits at the table and the phone starts to ring. Her friends drop by and want to talk. They want to do their homework together, but that seems a little like cheating to me—they seem to be just copying off each other's paper. I've had it! I finally said no phone and told her to stay in her room for an hour. If she doesn't get her homework done, it's not because I allowed her to play instead."

"To 'friend,' or not to 'friend'? That is the question." "Friend." That is the answer. The Caine Learning Institute explores twelve brain-based principles of learning in the book *12 Brain/ Mind Learning Principles in Action*. Principle 2 states that "all students learn more effectively when their social nature and need for relationship are engaged and honored." But "friend" with healthy ground rules.

Make Homework Time Enjoyable

When your children ask to study with friends, encourage them. Serve milk and cookies or popcorn and hot chocolate. Sit them around your dining table. Watch and listen as they all do their homework together. Place all your children around the same table; allow the older children to help the younger ones. This provides you with an invaluable opportunity to watch your children interact socially, to know their friends, and to hear their thinking processes.

If they digress and socialize, allow it—just set a time limit. Usually they will talk personally and giggle for a while, then return to their homework without your having to intervene. If they study in the bedroom, you miss out on the benefits of eavesdropping, and their digressions last longer.

Consider the following powerful reasons for studying together—so powerful, in fact, that I suggest you even have your "loners" study with friends at least once a week.

Remember that Talking Is Learning

Consider the following learning techniques:

- Speak or write information as you read it.
- Explain it to someone else.

Those who study with friends talk more as they study. When they get stuck, they explain things to one another. When they disagree over an answer, they argue about it. In the process, they learn more than one approach for arriving at an answer. When none of them can figure out how to resolve a problem, they all know that the problem was hard. They can confidently ask a question in class, knowing they won't be laughed at. All of these steps actually enhance the level of learning that occurs.

 It is better to solve one problem five different ways than to solve five different problems.—George Polya

Studying Together Reinforces a Commitment to Learning

Those who study with friends send out an unspoken message: "I do my homework. I try to learn. I take learning seriously.

Everybody does his homework." Even if they gripe about it, they are supporting one another socially in the act of learning. These children are not as likely to give in to school pressure when they are called "school boy" or "school girl" if they study (yes, sadly, those are "bad" labels in the eyes of children). According to researchers Treisman and Hodgkinson, the children who are most likely to drop out of high school and college are those who don't know how to form an academic support community around themselves in order to conquer difficult coursework.

Studying with Friends Involves More Senses

Consider the following learning principles:

- Use many senses to increase learning.
- Explain it to someone else.
- Personalize so you will remember.
- Express it two or more ways.

The more of ourselves we involve in learning, the more likely learning will occur (see Chapter 20, and Appendix A for a list of Learning Theories). That is why we teach children to write, draw, take notes, and rehearse—it involves more than one modality. When friends do homework together, they discuss answers. Talking is a kinesthetic process. According to Ricki Linksman's article "The Fine Line Between ADHD and Kinesthetic Learners," many children are diagnosed with attention deficit disorders when in reality they are kinesthetic learners. They need body movement in order to learn.

The most powerful way to learn is to teach something to someone else. Studying with friends allows your children to do that. For more information on the benefits of studying in a group, visit *www.kaganonline.com* or *www.co-operation.org*.

 The most powerful way to learn is to teach something to someone else.

The "no phone calls during homework" policy is a good one . . . unless the calls are about how to do the homework. However, one ten-minute purely social phone call is a great reward for one hour of study or one completed assignment.

See if your school offers a homework hotline to help when your children get stuck. Also, ask that the first few minutes of homework sessions be quiet—students learn more if they think about the problems a few minutes before they jump into a discussion.

·············· REFLECTION ··············

We experimented one summer with group discussions as a routine part of a math class. I videotaped interviews with the groups who had studied together—talking to one group at a time, behind closed doors, to get their comments for evaluation. They unanimously enjoyed studying in groups. When I asked why, each group gave a version of "Because I never made a fool of myself in front of the whole class."

Discussing coursework is a powerful way to learn. It also builds student confidence, enabling students to participate more actively in class. When students participate, teachers assume they want to learn. When teachers assume students want to learn, they reach out more often to offer help. It's a true win-win!

4

She Doesn't Remember from One Day to the Next

"My daughter is very bright, but sometimes she worries me. I'll help her with a subject and think she understands. Later we'll go over something similar or review what we had studied, and she doesn't remember. Could something serious be wrong?"

This could point to something serious, and certainly you should share this with your doctor during routine physical exams. But most serious learning difficulties are discovered relatively early in a child's life, and this problem could also result from a number of minor, and easily corrected, issues.

To help you discover the culprit, let me share a personal story with you.

One afternoon, a friend who disagreed with something I said commented, "Well, Sharon, I think you're wrong, but you have the right to do what you want to and I'll support you in it."

Such a polite disagreement; such a major reaction! After hanging up the phone, I spent about an hour arguing with him in my mind. Finally I thought, "This isn't like me! I believe people have a right to different viewpoints; I knew he would disagree, and I still think I made the right decision. What's wrong?"

I recounted my day and realized that it was mid-afternoon and I hadn't eaten anything all day. I'm hypoglycemic. I had an early dinner, and the whole world seemed better.

What does this have to do with children and homework? Usually the problem in school isn't intellectual.

When children aren't achieving the way they should, there is always a reason. Reasons are myriad, but they always have a root cause. The root cause may be physical, emotional, intellectual, or spiritual. Until you find the root cause, you are dealing with symptoms, or "putting a Band-Aid on the problem." When you discover the root, you can solve, resolve, or compensate for it. This concept is studied in depth in my SCORE *Staff Development Guide.*

 Until you find the root cause, you are dealing with symptoms, or "putting a Band-Aid on the problem." When you discover the root, you can solve, resolve, or compensate for it.

Physical Problems Related to Learning

One evening, a counselor and friend helped Jeff with his homework. When they finished, he asked me if I had had Jeff's eyes checked recently. I responded, "Yes, I've had his eyes checked. Every time he says, 'Sometimes I can't see,' and the best pediatric ophthalmologist in Orange County says, 'Your eyes are fine.' I'm not wasting any more money having his eyes checked."

Our counselor responded, "Then I'd like for him to have a his brain waves tested."

I said, "I'll have his eyes checked!"

Realizing we weren't getting anywhere with our highly qualified ophthalmologist, however, I began searching for alternatives. A friend referred me to a behavioral optometrist who specialized in children with learning disorders. He found Jeff had an eye-muscle problem, one that intensifies with stress or fatigue.

Finding the right doctor brought therapy to compensate for the disorder. Realizing that Jeff's problem was related to fatigue helped us understand why his work was so inconsistent.

Our physical being includes general health, not just appearance. Does your child perform better in the morning or afternoon? Some vision problems intensify with fatigue. Blood sugar varies throughout the day. Some of our children are just "morning people."

Does your child have difficulty sitting still for long periods of time? In the classroom, this includes children who wander around the room. Students who can't seem to sit still may be searching for meaning because their eyes or ears aren't working right.

Does your child perform better or worse after eating? Both low blood sugar and high blood sugar impair short-term memory. Food allergies can trigger learning problems. Learning is related to nutrition.

Normal childhood illnesses can affect learning.

In fact, learning is related to everything that affects our bodies. Let's examine a few possibilities.

Vision

Obviously, vision plays a major role in education. If your children are better at talking than they are at writing, an eye-hand coordination problem may be the culprit. As in Jeff's case, some health problems show up or intensify during stress, resulting in high classwork grades but low performance on tests. When Jeff was having problems, the Whittier Vision Center was life-changing (*www.optometrists.org/DrSpiro*). Other parents have found help from *Reading By the Colors* by Helen Irlen of the Irlen Institute (*www.irleninstitute.com*).

Children with eye-hand coordination problems may qualify to have exams read aloud to them. They may qualify for books on tape. Ask your doctor for referrals; ask your school for support; contact the Department of Rehabilitation; contact the Braille Institute (*www.brailleinstitute.org*).

Ophthalmologists deal with eye disease; optometrists deal with eye function; behavioral optometrists deal with eye muscle coordination; neurologists, among other things, deal with neurological system disorders that sometimes manifest themselves in visual problems.

According to the Optometric Extension Program Foundation, the following are possible signs of vision problems:

- Holding a book very close to the face (only 7 or 8 inches away)
- Holding the head at an extreme angle to the book when reading
- Covering one eye when reading
- Squinting when doing near vision work
- Having constant poor posture when working close
- Moving the head back and forth while reading instead of moving only eyes
- Having a poor attention span
- Getting drowsy after prolonged work less than arm's length away
- Taking longer than it should to do homework requiring reading
- Occasionally or persistently reporting blurred or double vision while reading or writing
- Reporting blurred or double vision only when work is hard
- Losing place when moving gaze from desk work to chalkboard, or when copying from text to notebook
- Using a marker to keep place when reading
- Writing at an uphill or downhill angle
- Writing with irregular letter or word spacing
- Reversing letters (b for d) or words (saw for was)
- Repeatedly omitting "small" words
- Rereading or skipping words or lines unknowingly
- Failing to recognize the same word in the next sentence
- Misaligning digits in columns of numbers
- Having headaches after reading or doing near work
- Blinking excessively when doing near work, but not otherwise
- Rubbing eyes during or after short periods of reading

- Having declining comprehension as reading continues
- Failing to visualize (can't describe what he has been reading about)

Reprinted with permission of the Optometric Extension Program © 2006, all rights reserved, *www.oep.org.*

Hearing and Speech

We parents sometimes hurt our own children by not facing our fears. Several of my friends have had children who show signs of hearing loss. One major sign appears early: most hard of hearing children have trouble speaking. They may talk or yell loudly with no sense of appropriate volume, or it may seem as though they have developed their own foreign language— they may make sounds or moans rather than speak words, or talk fluently but omit certain sounds.

In almost every case, when someone asks "Have you had his ears checked?" the response is "Oh, he's very smart. He's just stubborn. He hears what he wants to hear."

 The longer you wait to get help, the harder she will have to work to catch up.

Being smart and having a hearing problem are two different things. If you suspect a problem with hearing, immediately ask your pediatrician for a referral to a pediatric audiologist or contact the school district to request testing. In California, if you suspect a problem that will impact learning, children qualify for school health screening beginning at age three. Don't wait until your child starts school; contact your local school district to ask how early you can schedule a preliminary screening. For more information, contact the American Speech-Language-Hearing Association at *www.asha.org* (under "The Public," click "Speech, Language & Swallowing," then "Development") or the National Institute on Deafness and Other Communication Disorders at *www.nidcd.nih.gov* (under "Health Information," click "Hearing, Ear Infections, and Deafness").

Hearing loss is not likely to improve with age. Early diagnosis makes early intervention possible. Some problems may be solved completely, while others can be lifelong issues. If your child has a hearing impairment, the longer you wait to get help, the harder she will have to work to catch up.

If your child is mispronouncing some words, he may need speech therapy. The sounds for l, s, r, v, z, ch, sh, and th are commonly mispronounced. If your child is approaching school age and still having trouble with these sounds, it's time for a checkup.

Nutrition

A student who skips breakfast will not perform at maximum capacity because short-term memory is impaired by low blood sugar.

A child on a sugar high will not perform at maximum capacity because short-term memory is also impaired by high blood sugar.

Be sure to send nutritious snacks with your children if their lunch hour is late in the day or they don't have a nutrition break. Never insist that your child do homework before he can eat; rather, make food a normal part of studying and homework. In these days of epidemic childhood obesity, it is especially important to make their snacks healthy.

Certain foods (such as fish oils and blueberries) are considered to be "brain food" because they are rich in omega-3 fatty acids and antioxidants. Dr. Amen, in his book *Making a Good Brain Great*, tells us that "whatever is good for your heart is also good for your brain." He recommends a diet balanced with protein, good fats, and carbohydrates.

Allergies

Allergies can inhibit learning. Some children react to certain foods. Begin keeping track of what your child eats, and when, to determine if diet is affecting performance. Environmental allergies can compromise your child's ability to listen attentively.

Medications and Drugs

List and review side effects for all medications that your child is taking, both prescriptions and over-the-counter. Discuss these and your observations of learning difficulties with your doctor.

As inconceivable as it may seem, no family is immune to the possibility of substance abuse. Any major change in behavior is a sign that something is wrong. If you notice conspicuous changes in personality or behavior, look immediately for signs of alcohol, drugs, premature sexual activity, or depression.

Some common symptoms of substance abuse include:

- Excessive fatigue
- Bloodshot or glazed eyes
- Chronic cough
- Extreme mood swings
- Personality changes
- Drop in grades
- Loss of interest in learning
- New friends with different values
- Change in style of dress
- Emotional withdrawal
- Outbursts of anger

 Any major change in behavior is a sign that something is wrong.

Some of the warning signs listed above can also be signs of other problems. Parents may recognize signs of trouble but should not be expected to make the diagnosis. An effective way for parents to show care and concern is to openly discuss the use and possible abuse of alcohol and other drugs with their children.

Consulting a physician to rule out physical causes of the warning signs is a good first step. This might be followed or accompanied by a comprehensive evaluation by a child and adolescent psychiatrist.

Exercise

Does your child get adequate exercise? As concisely stated by Dr. Amen in *The Secrets of Successful Students*, "Exercise increases the production of endorphins in your body. Endorphins are the chemicals your body produces naturally that, among other things, add to your sense of well-being. Increasing your mental stamina and self-confidence will help you study better." Make sure your children are exercising their bodies as well as their minds.

Sleep

Does your child get a good night's sleep? Are there sleep problems that you observe?

Although every child is unique, most sleep researchers agree on the following norms:

- Children three to six years old need ten to twelve hours of sleep a night.
- Children seven to twelve years old need ten to eleven hours per night.
- Children twelve to eighteen years old need at least eight to nine and one-half hours of sleep per night.

Some researchers studying the sleep patterns of teens have commented that teenagers need more sleep than these norms, but they don't get it. Most children don't get enough sleep, and lack of sleep affects learning.

Emotional Problems Related to Learning

We train our tutors in both learning theory and grief recovery. One of our tutors worked with Amy. Amy was distracted and acted differently than she had in the past. Our tutor began talking with her to discover why there was a major change in her behavior. She soon found the culprit: Amy's grandfather had just died, and she couldn't get to his funeral. Knowing this, the tutor was able to incorporate Amy's loss into her homework. Her English assignment became a tribute to her grandfather. Amy drew a picture of him with his walker, outlined by her poem. She earned a B on her assignment and learned a healthy way to grieve.

I received an e-mail some time ago reviewing salaries. It gave the U.S. president's salary, professional athletes' salaries, famous actors' and actresses' salaries. The final entry was the salary of Bill Gates, the highest-paid person in America. The e-mail concluded, "Marry a nerd."

We understand that, but our children don't. They are desperate for peer approval. If performance wanes, find out what is going on emotionally, both at home and in the hours your child is away from home. You may find the culprit.

Children are all different and all wear their feelings in different ways, but all children are affected when emotional pressures rise. Emotions can enhance or thwart learning. If your children are having difficulty learning, try to discover if there are emotional causes.

Are other children teasing them about something? Are they embarrassed about something? A sensitive child whose shoe has a hole in it will spend much energy trying to remember not to cross his or her legs lest the hole be discovered. This is energy spent at the expense of learning.

Children can be extremely cruel to one another. It is not uncommon for children to take off glasses the moment they leave home rather than face a taunt about being "four eyes."

If your child is being teased by peers, it will show up in the classroom. Sadly, sometimes children are teased because they're smart: "You're a nerd." "Teacher's pet!"

A little anxiety actually enhances learning; severe anxiety shuts down our capacity to retrieve information from our memory bank. In times of severe anxiety, mnemonic devices, laughter, and movement help retrieve information (see Chapters 11 and 18).

Does your child freeze during a test? If so, teaching relaxation techniques, visual imagery, and right-brain trigger points will help resolve the problem.

 A little anxiety enhances learning; severe anxiety shuts down our capacity to retrieve information from our memory bank.

You might also look at how your child's personality matches that of the teacher. A sensitive child who feels (justified or not) that the teacher is picking on him can't learn efficiently.

While we're looking at reactions, look at your mornings. When there is dissention in the household, a child may go to school overcome with either anger or fear. Both of these emotions can short-circuit learning.

Grief

Have you recently made a major change in your life? Moving, death, divorce, and serious illnesses cause us to grieve. Grief reactions cause a child to spend energy coping—at the expense of learning. A child's first experience with grief is usually with the death of a pet. Average grieving time is two years. If children bury grief, it can last much longer. While grieving, children may need more of your time helping with homework.

We had several deaths in our family when Jeff was just a toddler. Before our time of trauma, when I would give him a paper and crayons, he would scribble over the entire page. In the aftermath of our crises, when I gave him paper and crayons, he would draw in a tiny, postage-stamp size space on the corner of the page. He pulled his world in to where it was manageable to him.

When you have experienced a recent loss, move, or trauma, you may observe the following changes in your child's behavior as he endeavors to cope with his new life reality. These behavior changes are normal and simply a sign that your child needs some extra nurturing:

- The way they write or color is different.
- The content or style of their drawing changes.
- Their frustration level increases.
- They become more shy or more talkative.
- They become more clingy or withdrawn.
- Their eating habits change.
- Their sense of humor changes.
- They develop illnesses or fears.
- They are periodically afraid to go to sleep.
- They are more childish or more mature than is normal for their age.

Negative emotions cause the child to work much harder to learn because so much energy is used to suppress feelings of anger, inferiority, guilt, and fear.

Of course, you can't shield your child from life; instead, you must help him cope with it. If you suspect your child is underachieving because of an emotional issue, seek counseling. Spend homework time sitting beside him, listening when he needs to talk . . . gently prodding.

Here are some symptoms that, as I teach in my workshop "Crisis, Grief, and Loss . . . and How to Help Your Students Through It," indicate children need extra help with their grief. If you observe these symptoms, seek help even if you can't identify the immediate cause:

- Drawings of death or violence
- Cruelty to other children
- Cruelty to animals
- Phantom or copycat illnesses
- Facial tics or body twitches
- Eyes that cross or won't focus
- Obsessive behavior
- Lethargy or hyperactivity

Spiritual Problems Related to Learning

"Tell me about your parents. What do they think about your wanting to be a doctor?"

In a split second, Mario bounced into his parent routine: "They say, 'Get that silly idea out of your head, honey! We can't afford to send you to medical school!'"

As I got to know both Mario and his parents, I discovered a great communication gap in this statement. Mario heard "Get your head out of the clouds! You're not smart enough to be a doctor!" His parents meant, "You are so bright, and we are inadequate!" Both Mario and his parents, in this instance, were suffering from a low sense of worth.

We normally think of the spiritual as being just our religious beliefs, and certainly our religious preferences are spiritual. But in reality, the spiritual is much more. Every person has a spiritual part, whether or not he or she is religious. Our spiritual self includes that which we hide except to our few best and most trusted friends. It consists of our dreams, goals, and values.

 We cannot live at dissonance with ourselves.

I believe that self-esteem is enhanced or damaged most often at the level of the spirit. In the illustration above, Mario's parents were unwittingly (and certainly unintentionally) robbing him of a dream. We need to learn, instead, how to dream with our children—ask them questions: Why do you want to be a doctor? What kind of doctor you want to be? Who is your favorite doctor? What do you like about him?

You may be thinking "But it's true; I can't afford that!" Fortunately, we live in a world that values education; help is available for the child with a big dream and tiny budget. Children need your approval and encouragement far more than your money.

Has your child recently had a disappointment? Our spiritual self includes our dreams. A dream dies hard. Has your child recently tried for something and failed? A potential athlete, for example, who pitched the winning run for the other team might believe that his future is over. If so, it may affect classroom learning until he dares to dream again.

 Find their dream, then become their greatest fan.

Is there something going on that would tempt him to compromise his values? A student who is doing something that goes against personal values will suffer guilt that will distract from the process of learning. Our values are a part of our spiritual self. We cannot live at dissonance with ourselves. If your child is doing something that his inner self says is wrong, it will affect all aspects of his life and will short-circuit learning.

Is something happening in your home that causes her to question values? Often when there is a divorce, the child is angry because divorce is not "acceptable." In a child's mind, the very people who taught the sanctity of marriage have violated it, causing an internal value conflict.

A person who is pursuing a parent's dream rather than his own will suffer lowered self-esteem.

A student without a career goal will not be as diligent in studying as one who knows where she's headed.

If your children are struggling, encourage their natural interests and talents. Help them discover what they are good at and what they enjoy doing. Help them explore different career areas. Find their dream, then become their greatest fan.

I once held a workshop with parents where I asked, "What are your dreams for your children?" Dreams filled the room, one after another. All the parents had lavish dreams for their children.

I then asked, "What are your children's dreams for themselves?" The room was silent. Finally, one parent said, "I don't think my daughter has a dream."

I responded, "I could spend five minutes with your daughter and would probably know her dream. I'm going to do something better, though. I'm going to teach you how to find it."

Here's the process. I wish I could teach you in person!

- Ask your child what she wants to do when she grows up.
- Say, "*That's wonderful. Tell me more about it.*"
- Ask who she knows in that profession.
- Ask if there is a specialty area in which she is interested.
- Ask...ask...ask. Ask her a million questions and cheer her for every answer.
- Tell her you'll do everything within your power to help her reach her dream.
- Do everything within your power to help her reach her dream.

In my SCORE program, we call this process "petting the dream." We thought we invented it but were recently humbled when we ran across a quote by Harry Truman: "The best way to give advice to your children is to find out what they want and advise them to do it."

Intellectual Problems Related to Learning

I once looked at Jeff's test paper after he had failed an exam and didn't know why. It became obvious as I looked. I commented to the teacher, "Wow, now I see what is happening. You tested deep, and he studied wide." The teacher did not understand so I responded, "You tested cause and effect: in the story, this caused this, which created this effect, which caused this to happen." The teacher nodded in agreement. He had, indeed, tested for the detail. I continued, "Jeff studied 'wide' and saw relationships: 'this happened in the story, which caused this reaction." Jeff had thought, "My friend Hector has that problem. He's working on it in a study group.'"

When we think of school problems, the intellectual area is normally where we look. We wonder if our children are "smart," or of "average intelligence," or "slow learners." These labels are usually destructive. Every child in school has the intellectual capacity to learn. Those who struggle because of a learning disorder can be diagnosed and can learn to manage it. An intellectual problem can include a child's approach to learning, but it does not include the capacity to learn.

When a child completes the homework, studies, and then performs poorly on an exam, it is time to request a parent conference. Don't wait; check with the teacher.

When a child studies one way and is tested another, it may cause confusion. There was a mismatch between the way Jeff studied and the way he was tested. He studied themes; he was tested on details. Because he is by nature thematic, he has to work to see the details, or study with a friend when he has a teacher who gives objective exams.

Is there a mismatch between the way the teacher is teaching and the way your child learns? If a teacher teaches details and your child learns in abstracts, there may be a mismatch. Help your child move from abstract to concrete as you help with homework.

 An intellectual problem can include a child's approach to learning, but it does not include the capacity to learn.

Is the teacher teaching in a visual manner, but your child needs tactile input in order to learn? If so, help your daughter learn to take notes in class. Taking notes is a tactile skill that will enrich her level of learning.

Is the teacher teaching in an auditory manner, but your child needs kinesthetic input in order to learn? If so, take the content from the classroom and help your child talk it through or walk it through or act it through.

When a teacher teaches one way and tests another, there is a mismatch that confuses some children. For example, some teachers teach concepts but give the textbook exam. Textbook exams usually test for detail.

An intellectual problem is something that can be solved by using a different technique or a different structure. When a child has poor study habits and doesn't retain information, we have an intellectual problem. This is the easiest one to correct; we teach her study skills. An intellectual problem that shows up in learning could be:

- Poor study habits on the part of the student, in which case we empower him with study and learning strategies.
- Test anxiety on the part of the student, in which case we teach her to take several deep breaths and focus before beginning a test.
- A mismatch between a teacher's teaching style and a student's learning style. Usually in these cases we train the teacher to teach to every learning style in every class, every day. Often, we invite parents and students to sit in on the training as well.

More on this topic is in the chapters that follow. In a nutshell, we need to train our students to start learning from their point of strength, but to study from different perspectives.

Work the Circle

In staff-development sessions with teachers struggling to help students learn, I teach them to "work the circle." If we think of life's balance as a circle, with our physical, our emotional, our spiritual, and our intellectual beings each as a portion of the circle, ideally all four parts of our circle are healthy and equal.

We are interconnected. When a school problem arises, look for a physical root cause—for example, is there a vision problem? If that doesn't work, look at emotions. Is your child being teased? If this is not the solution, look for an intellectual cause. Perhaps there is a mismatch between teaching style and learning style. If not, check out values. Is your child giving in to peer pressure in some area?

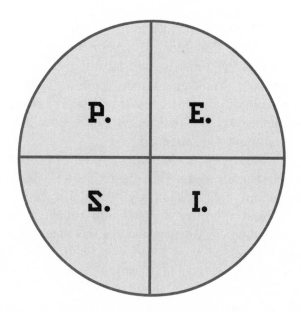

Continue to "work the circle" until you find a resolution:

Intellectual: Try studying with them.

Emotional: Remind them that they're smart. They especially need to be reassured of this after they've failed an exam.

Spiritual: Have they had a major disappointment lately? Maybe they tried out for the cheerleading squad or soccer team and didn't make it. If so, you need to listen to them and assure them they will have another chance.

Physical: Do they have food allergies that interfere with learning?

Intellectual: "Perhaps you studied concepts, but the teacher gave an objective test. Let's memorize the names, dates, and places in this story." If this works, you have found a root cause. If it doesn't, you have used a temporary solution, a Band-Aid. (Remember, Band-Aids are good.)

Emotional: "Did you freeze on the test? Let's study using mnemonic devices." (They create a right-brain trigger, helping to reduce test anxiety). If this works, you have found a root cause. If it doesn't, you have used a Band-Aid. (Remember, Band-Aids are good.)

Spiritual: "What do you want to be when you grow up?" Spend some time dreaming with your son or daughter. In SCORE, we call this process "petting the dream." When children know their goal, they are more focused in their studies, even in seemingly unrelated classes. If this works, you have found a root cause. If it doesn't, you have used a Band-Aid. (Remember, Band-Aids are good.)

Physical: "You knew it; you gave me the answers when we worked together last night. That means it's in there; we'll find a way to get it out. Tell me about your test." You are seeking differences in time of day (e.g., before or after lunch), wondering if food plays a role. If so, you have found a root cause. If it doesn't, you have used a Band-Aid. (Remember, Band-Aids are good.)

If nothing has worked, you are still seeking a root cause. Work the circle again.

As you continue to work the circle, try charting what your child is eating to see if certain foods cause a reaction. Intervene in a different area each time until you discover the root cause. You will know when you have found the root cause because grades will improve almost immediately. Until then, continue to use the Band-Aids.

Life Balance and Depression

We need to achieve life balance. If we abuse our physical being, pretty soon the void created by that abuse spills over into our emotional, then our intellectual, then our spiritual sides. If we ignore the emotional dimension of our lives, pretty soon that void causes us to malfunction intellectually, spiritually, and physically—we develop illnesses such as depression.

Depression is a strange animal. When we think of depression, we think of inertia and self-destructive behaviors. Certainly these are symptoms. But depression can also mask itself as hyperactivity: "I've got to keep running because if I stop, I have to think. If I think, I have to feel. If I feel, I have to cry. If I cry, I can never quit so I've got to keep running."

In general, extremes in behavior may be a sign of childhood depression. Ask yourself, "Is this normal for a child this age?"

If the answer is "No," or "I'm not sure," talk with your physician about it. For example, "Is it normal for a 6-year-old child to sleep only six hours a night?" The answer is "No." Talk with your physician. "Is it normal for a 6-year-old child to be too tired to eat when he comes home from school?" The answer is "No." Talk with your physician. "Is it normal for a 6-year-old to have fights two or three times a week with her best friend?" The answer is "Sometimes." Watch for other symptoms before taking action.

 As parents, it is important that we observe rather than diagnose.

If you suspect depression, consult your physician. If your child exhibits self-destructive behavior, expresses thoughts of suicide (in speech, drawings, or writings), run, don't walk, to the nearest source of help. Sadly, even young children may commit suicide. It is the third leading cause of death in teenagers (according to an American Academy of Child and Adolescent Psychiatry 2004 report that can be found at *www.aacap.org*).

As parents, it is important that we observe rather than diagnose. Tell your physician what you observe; the same symptoms may point to any number of problems.

According to the American Association of Child and Adolescent Psychiatry, if one or more of these signs of depression persists, parents should seek help:

- Frequent sadness, tearfulness, crying
- Hopelessness
- Decreased interest in activities; or inability to enjoy previously favorite activities
- Persistent boredom; low energy
- Social isolation, poor communication
- Low self-esteem and guilt
- Extreme sensitivity to rejection or failure
- Increased irritability, anger, or hostility
- Difficulty with relationships

- Frequent complaints of physical illnesses such as headaches and stomachaches
- Frequent absences or poor performance in school
- Poor concentration
- A major change in eating and/or sleeping patterns
- Talk of or efforts to run away from home
- Thoughts or expressions of suicide or self destructive behavior

·········· REFLECTION ··········

When Jeff entered college, the old patterns reappeared. He loved his classes, told me how much he was learning, and always received grades much lower than he thought he had earned. He could never predict how well he would do on a test.

I treated it as poor study habits; he enrolled in a study skills class and received tutoring. I treated it as test anxiety; we got counseling. He had reached the point of academic probation when I called the learning center at his college:

"Jeff is struggling, and I don't know how to help him."

"You're already doing more than most parents. Maybe you need to let go. Maybe he needs to experience failure so he will take responsibility for himself."

(Wow! You should have seen my feathers ruffle!) "You're talking about co-dependency. I was married to an alcoholic. I know how to pull the plug. If there were anything in me that thought he was goofing off, I would have no problem ceasing to write you tuition checks; I don't like to part with my money! But I think he's doing everything he knows how to do and failing tests anyway. If that's true, I owe him everything I can do to help."

"Does he have a learning disability?"

"No, but he has this vision problem . . ."

Interesting that I am an educator, and I struggled with Jeff through his primary grades because of his eye-hand coordination difficulties, but I did not recognize it as a learning disability. When I said, "He has this vision problem . . ." the University said, "How fast can you fax us the medical report?"

Within one hour of their receipt of the medical report, they had turned things around for Jeff. Because of his vision problem, he was allowed to have his exams read aloud to him. With the exams read aloud, he could finally see that his eyes were not tracking; he was literally seeing white spots on the page. Where his eyes crossed, he saw a double image. Our brains cannot comprehend a double image so it translates them as blanks. Once he could understand what was going on, he cooperated more readily. He passed the exams, brought up his GPA, and graduated.

5

I've Told Him a Dozen Times!

"I've told him a dozen times, and he still doesn't understand! Sometimes I wonder if he even listens; other times, I'm afraid something is wrong. I've even taken him in to have his ears checked!"

Sometimes we explain things to our children and ask if they understand. After years of working with students, I can confidently say one thing: They *always* say they understand. It must be biologically impossible to admit to confusion. But . . . they don't *always* understand. They don't know they don't understand, however, until they try to explain it to you. After each concept, then, ask your children to repeat what they've learned to you.

Learn about Our Marvelous Brains

An understanding of how the brain functions is one of the most exciting discoveries of recent years. It has far-reaching implications as we help our children learn. Everything we have ever learned or experienced is stored somewhere in our brains; it is more powerful than our greatest computer.

Our brain is incredibly complex. Part of our brain controls logical, orderly, sequential learning; it stores an amazing amount of data and information. Usually this is housed in our left lobe, so we refer to people who are logical as "left-brain learners." Another part of our brain controls spatial, relational, and interactional functions. Usually these are controlled in our right lobe, so we call people who are creative "right-brain learners." Of course, barring brain damage, our entire brain works in concert all the time.

Further Reading on Brain Research

Brain research is one of the most exciting aspects of teaching in today's world. For further reading on the subject, check out the following books and Web sites:

1. *Making a Good Brain Great* and *The Secrets of Successful Students* by Daniel G. Amen, MD
2. *Multiple Intelligences in the Classroom* by Thomas Armstrong
3. *12 Brain/Mind Learning Principles in Action* by Renate Nummela Caine, Geoffrey Caine, Carol Lynn McClintic, and Karl J. Klimek and *MindShifts* by Geoffrey Caine, Renate Nummela Caine, and Sam Crowell
4. *Frames of Mind: The Theory of Multiple Intelligences* by Howard Gardner
5. *www.yale.edu/rjsternberg* for information on Robert J. Sternberg's research

Some children naturally prefer to learn through logic and the acquisition of facts. Others learn best through feelings, concepts, or relationships. Before we began to understand brain function, most of our teaching focused on acquisition of information. As a result, an artistic or reflective student often had difficulty in school—not in learning, but in translating what was learned into typical vehicles for measuring what learning had occurred. To an artistic or reflective student, learning facts and data seems both boring and unimportant.

We have spent centuries endeavoring to separate emotions from learning, yet brain research reported by Caine and Caine is now suggesting that learning cannot occur outside the realm of our emotions. The way we approach teaching has been revolutionized by recent brain research.

Start at Their Point of Strength

If your children have difficulty understanding a concept, work with them at their point of strength.

I was trying to tutor a student in an independent study program. Independent study students are in big trouble in their schools. They are no longer incarcerated for whatever offenses they have committed, but they are also no longer welcome back to their previous high school. Most of these students have an "attitude."

I sat down with a student working on geometry and said to him, "So . . . are you good at math?" One of our keys when working with students is that you develop a relationship with them before you delve into the curriculum. That way they are more accepting of your pointers.

His response was "No, I stink at it."

I said, "Wow! You are doing geometry; how can you stink at math?"

He said, "I just do. I don't understand it; I don't know what I am doing."

I said, "So, tell me what you are into," and he responded, "Skateboarding."

"Skateboarding! You mean you can go down those hills and come back up and land on your feet instead of your watussi?"

"Yeah," he said, and his eyes lit up.

"Do you know how to figure out how fast you have to be going so you can actually make the jump?"

"Yeah."

"Do you know how to figure out what angle to skate so you can get to the bottom and back up at rocket speed?"

After we had talked a while about skateboarding, I patted him on the shoulder and said, "That's geometry. Never tell me again that you are not good in math."

He actually smiled.

When your children don't understand what they read, ask about something they enjoy:

"If you were singing a song, how do you think you would sing this story?"

"If you were drawing a picture, how would you draw this math problem?"

"If you were text-messaging a friend, how would you describe this historical event?"

"If you were writing the book, what would you write about this science experiment?"

When they reach comprehension, go back to the homework and help them draw the parallel.

Use Their Natural Intelligence

Researcher Howard Gardner revolutionized the way we think about learning with his theory of multiple intelligences, introduced in the late 1980s. From that theory, many slogans have emerged:

Don't ask how smart is he, but how is he smart.

Every child is 100% smart.

A smart person is someone who can build on strengths and compensate for weaknesses.

The Strong National Museum of Play in Rochester, New York (*www.strongmuseum.org*) labels those various intelligences "smart." For example, having logical and mathematical intelligence is being Number Smart. Using the descriptors from the National Museum of Play, they are described below. Howard Gardner's terms are written in italics below and repeated after each type of "smart."

Word Smart

Was your child born talking? Can your child communicate well with words? Your child probably has a well-developed *linguistic intelligence*. If that is the case, he will respond to reading text and then trying to explain it in his own words, or to listening to something that is explained and then reexplaining it to you.

This is the intelligence most often used in school settings. If they struggle, have them read a passage; then explain it to you.

Start where they are strong, and use that strength to help them compensate for their weakness. Once they grasp the concept, convert it into the language used in their classrooms.

Number Smart

A number-smart child has a high level of *logical and mathematical intelligence*. Number-smart people usually tend to argue loudly because they have a built-in sense of logic. Number-smart children have to win an argument. Number-smart children are the ones who say, "Why should I do that fifty times? I've already proven I know how."

Number-smart children who are struggling to learn will respond to sequences, to steps: do this first, this second, this third, this fourth. Breaking something down into its parts will help a number-smart child gain understanding.

Nature Smart

A nature smart child is one with a well-developed, intuitive affinity for the world around him: *naturalist intelligence*. These are the children who would rescue a homeless puppy. They are the children who take a spider outside so it can continue to live. They are the children who seem to have been born with a "green thumb." They easily relate to other cultures, seeing both the differences from and similarities to their own.

Unfortunately, this is not an intelligence that is often validated or used in the classroom. If you have a nature-smart child who is struggling in the classroom, use examples from nature to help her understand: "Remember how our puppy barked and jumped up and down and ran around in circles because he was so excited to see us? He must have been lonely while we were gone. That's probably how Dorothy felt in

The Wizard of Oz. She liked her new friends, but she must have been frightened and lonely to be in a strange place." Or "You know how we can count tree rings to tell how old a tree is? That's a little like math. Imagine that every ring is five years. How old would a tree with three rings be?"

People Smart

These are the children with intuitive *interpersonal intelligence.* They are your babies who were born eager to meet new people. These are the small children who can walk up to someone and talk about anything. These are the children whose friends come to them for wise advice; they seem to be gifted in relationships.

If you have a child who is people smart and struggling in the classroom, talk about his work or invite friends from school to study with him. Allow this child to explore ideas and problems through conversation. If he struggles to understand, let him talk. Don't correct him; let him correct himself. Make suggestions, and have him "brainstorm" with you. When he reaches the point of understanding, validate him. Pat him on the back and say, *"Yes—you've got it now! Write that down really fast before you forget it."*

Picture Smart

Picture-smart children have an intuitive *visual/spatial intelligence.* They are the children who know how they want to decorate their rooms. They are the babies who explored pictures more than people or toys. They are the children who worked puzzles well because they could visualize how the little pieces fit into the whole. They may or may not be artistic, but they learn through images easier than through words.

If you have a child who is naturally picture smart, draw a picture for her that relates to what she is studying. Better yet, have her draw her own picture of what she reads. Read to her, then help her draw a picture. Unfortunately, picture-smart people aren't often validated in the classroom after they leave elementary school, so you may have to help her develop her self-esteem, especially as she gets into higher-level classes.

Body Smart

A body-smart child is someone born with *bodily kinesthetic intelligence.* They are often children who are well-coordinated and have a good grasp of their physical abilities. These children are also those who can't sit still; they are your wigglers, and being forced to sit still is like punishment to them. When they are told to sit still, be quiet, and listen in the classroom, it feels as though they are being tortured.

If you have a child who is body smart and struggling to learn, don't make her sit down when she gets home. Let her stand up to study; play a game of catch with her while she rehearses the information she needs to learn; allow her to walk in circles while she reads.

These children are good at multitasking—they can comfortably do two or three things at once. Their body needs to wiggle for their mind to work. If they are struggling with homework, let them move. Let them play while they talk it through. When they come up with the gold nugget, say, "*Good! Sit down fast and write that.*"

These children will need to learn to manage their kinesthetic intelligence in the classroom. Other chapters in this book will expand on the strategies they need in order to learn. Have them take creative notes (see Chapter 14) that allow them to get the wiggles out so they can sit down in the classroom. Remember that "body smartness" is not often valued in the classroom. When they comprehend, you may need to help them translate what they learned into the language of the classroom.

Music Smart

A music-smart person has a well-developed *musical/rhythmic intelligence.* As infants, music-smart children could sleep soundly with background noise. As elementary-school children, they created songs and sang them, usually with good pitch. They could march to a beat and clap their hands to a rhythm. Musical intelligence, however, is often undervalued after they leave elementary school. Music-smart children may be prodigies, or they may simply rhyme and rhythm their way through life.

If he is struggling with a concept, have him create a symphony that expresses the mood, the tone, of what he is trying to learn. If he is struggling to learn something fundamental, reduce it to the tune of *Itsy, Bitsy Spider* and have him fill in what he is trying to memorize to that tune. Singing information doesn't excuse him from functioning in the classroom intelligently; it empowers him. When you are constantly telling a music-smart person to sit down, be quiet, and write, you are devaluing his innate intelligence. He needs to feel good about his talent so he has the self-esteem to do other tasks.

Self Smart

Self-smart children are your little dreamers. They have a well developed *intrapersonal intelligence.* When they learn a new concept, they immediately go inside to personalize it to see how it relates to them. They might go off into a thought world; one thought triggers something that creates other thoughts and images in their minds.

This intelligence isn't always well developed in the classroom. If you have a child who has a high level of intrapersonal intelligence who is struggling to learn, have him journal about his assignments for a few minutes before doing homework. Periodically sit down with him, talking quietly about his assignment until he comes to a point of understanding. Then give him three minutes to write down what he just learned and how it relates to him. Validate him appropriately; then help him translate his understanding into the language of his classroom.

Future Smart

These children were born asking questions about the meaning of life. They have a well-developed, intuitive *existential intelligence.* As a small child, she probably asked a million questions you were hesitant to answer. She has an innate knowledge that the world is bigger than she is. She is constantly searching for clues to the universe.

If she struggles in the classroom, help her see how mathematics will help her in later life, and how coming up with several themes and viewpoints will help her gain understanding.

I used Howard Gardner's research to discuss the theory of multiple intelligences. Some researchers have expanded this concept to seventeen or more intelligences. To help you find strengths in your children, begin watching their behavior. What do they do well? What do they enjoy doing? What do they do that consumes their free time? Do they talk to friends on the phone, text-message, play computer games, play board games, read a book, listen to music, or shoot baskets?

Where they spend their time—where time seems to stand still for them—is probably the area of their natural intelligence and where their intuitive talent lies. Use that, whatever it is, to help them learn. If they enjoy using the computer, for example, and they are struggling to understand a concept, send them to the computer and give them ten minutes to either write out their frustration or find out everything they can about that topic. Then come back and revisit what they are struggling with, drawing illustrations from the point of view of their strengths.

Don't Talk—Involve

Now, back to the child who has been told a dozen times. Quit "telling" and start "involving." Students don't really learn something until they have processed it. Have them explain it to you. If they can do that, but still don't remember, the problem is often one of access. Using techniques that involve emotion, humor, art, or music have proven effective in reducing anxiety and providing a trigger to memory. Think of our brain as a giant computer; the "trigger" is either the file name or the icon. Once you can remember that, you can open the file and get out all the information you want!

We can help our children learn a concept by:

- Converting it into a picture
- Using a real object
- Reminding them of a past similar experience
- Having them imagine themselves teach it to someone else
- Acting it out in a skit
- Singing it to the tune of a familiar song
- Turning it into a rap
- Asking a question to which the information is the answer
- With friends, creating a group poem that teaches the concept

The list is endless! There is just one key . . . learning involves our entire being. Learning can—and should be—fun!

 Think of our brain as a giant computer.

Work for Content Mastery

Wherever you begin the understanding process, bring it back to the classroom. Say, "Remember when your teacher talked about laissez-faire leadership? . . . 'That's what we just drew a picture of.'"

REFLECTION

Grace, a sixth-grade teacher, taught a series of lessons on Egyptian pharaohs, which she called "the superstars of Egypt." While she gave her lecture, the students took class notes. They then converted those notes into pictures. In groups, they shared their pictures; then they took their notes and pictures home to be signed by their parents and returned the next day.

John, one of her problem students, did nothing through the first six superstars, but something got him excited about superstar number seven. He drew a picture and shared it with his classmates.

After class, John asked if he could borrow her class notes to take home that night so he could "draw cooler pictures." He had never acted remotely interested in anything before. She "kissed her notes good-bye," thinking she would never see them again, and handed them to John.

The next day he came in with all seven superstars completed and his parent's signature on the papers.

Grace was excited by his change in attitude. It lasted until time for him to take the test. When he reached question two, he made loud, obnoxious noises, threw his pen down, and quit working.

Her instinct was to throw him out of class, she was so tired of dealing with his belligerent behavior. "But," she thought, "I'll try one more thing." She handed John a blank sheet of paper and said, "Draw me what you remember from your notes."

She expected him to remember a little bit, but, to her surprise, he reproduced verbatim everything he had had in his notes. She said, "Now use this to answer these questions."

He said, "But isn't that cheating?"

She responded, "No, I just watched it come right out of your brain."

He used his picture notes to answer his test questions and made the first A+ of his life.

6

She Could Dawdle All Day

"I get so upset with her! I think she's in doing her homework, and when I check she's still at the same place she was when I left 30 minutes ago to start dinner! Sometimes she just sits and stares into space. She knows how to do the work, but getting it out of her is more work for me than for her! Help!"

Our wonderful little dreamers! Getting them to stay on task is a challenge, even for the most creative parent. Perhaps it will help if we understand their personalities. The concept of four personalities dates back to Hippocrates, more than 2,000 years ago. In discussing these learning preferences, I have chosen to use the Greek names he applied: Phlegmatic, Sanguine, Melancholy, and Choleric. The next four chapters examine learning based on personality type.

The Phlegmatic Personality: Concept-Oriented

About 12 percent of our children think in terms of concepts rather than details. They avoid conflict and seek peace. They were wonderful babies; they didn't care if they were on schedule or off, wet or dry. You could get them up in the middle of the night to show them off to Aunt Matilda, then put them back to bed where they would continue to sleep through the night.

They could entertain themselves for hours. If you weren't careful, you could neglect them.

In the classroom, however, these wonderful babies may turn into problem students. They daydream a lot. They ask off-the-wall questions. They begin a project one way, then digress and finish it another—or abandon it altogether and start something new. We worry about them for "avoidance behaviors"—the more they have to do, the more they seem to ignore it and think about something else.

Phlegmatics Are Daydreamers

Our Phlegmatic children are what we call divergent thinkers. One word reminds them of a dozen experiences related to that word, but not necessarily related to the lesson. They periodically spin off into their imaginations and don't even hear what the teacher is saying. They see the forest rather than the tree, the tree rather than the cell. They have vivid imaginations that carry them into worlds unknown. They are not often motivated for the sake of a high grade. To earn high grades, they need to build in reflective time. As they mature, they learn how to balance reflection and achievement.

Phlegmatics Are Storytellers

Our Phlegmatic children sometimes talk in circles. They start by exploring the many facets of an issue. They seem to be talking about something so irrelevant to the topic that we give up listening and think they don't know what they are talking about.

If we listen more closely, we will discover the way they think. They talk in circles. They may create an example that talks around the idea of what you were just working on. They would never intentionally hurt someone's feelings, so instead of "shooting straight" and "cutting to the chase," they try to figure out a way to say the same thing but soften the blow. Rather than tell you what they are thinking, they may tell a story that has the same theme as what they want to say.

When I deal with people who are frustrated trying to communicate with Phlegmatics, I suggest they quit listening to the first 50 words and listen to the last 50. After Phlegmatics have talked in circles, they get to the point.

Phlegmatics are so soft-spoken that they don't command our attention. When we quit listening to them, they feel devalued and begin to shut down emotionally. It is vitally important that we listen to them, that we hear what they have to say, and that we help them get around to focusing on key ideas.

For concept-oriented children to function effectively in the classroom, their divergent thinking patterns must be validated. You might say *"Yes, isn't it interesting how the Indians dance. For today, though, I want you to focus on the kind of food they ate"* rather than "What does dancing have to do with food?"

Phlegmatics See the Big Picture

Our Phlegmatic children are naturally gifted in the gestalt—the big picture. Did you ever try to work a jigsaw puzzle when you didn't have a picture of the pattern to follow? The tiny pieces could fit anywhere unless you know the patterns of the coloring. For Phlegmatics, focusing on the details of a lesson without knowing where it fits into the scheme of things is like working a jigsaw puzzle without knowing what you're trying to create. If you find them avoiding something, it might help to draw a picture of the concept, then explain to them the piece of the whole that they are working on now. Then help them know where to begin and how to proceed logically from one step to the next.

Phlegmatics Value Relationship

In teaching a class on personality, I asked the students to answer four questions about their personality. I peeked over their shoulders and saw that the Phlegmatics had their work done and had done it well. When it was their turn to report, I called on them. No one would come forward to share their answers. I tried every teaching tool I know to get someone to volunteer to report out. Nothing worked. Finally, I said, "Okay, everybody up." Twelve little Phlegmatic personalities got up and walked to the front of the room and lined up beside me.

I read the first question, "What stresses you?" The student at the end of the line whispered the answer into the next person's ear, who whispered it to the next. . . . Student number twelve whispered the answer in my ear, and I spoke it out to the class.

A Phlegmatic will never value accomplishment over relationship. A Phlegmatic student will take an F on an assignment before he or she will upstage a peer. In the Phlegmatic value system, everyone is equal so it is not okay to appear superior to a friend. For that reason, I do a lot of group work in the classroom. Group projects allow Phlegmatics to be a part of the group and to showcase their work without fear of making a friend look bad or setting themselves up as a class example.

 A Phlegmatic will never value accomplishment over relationship.

If you notice a change in personality, watch the tone in the classroom. If a Phlegmatic child doesn't feel valued in the classroom, learning becomes a struggle. Make sure their teachers connect with them at a personal level. It's as easy as asking the teacher to make a point of greeting them, by name, with a smile as they enter the classroom.

Phlegmatics Are Peacemakers

They shut down when conflict occurs. If you watch them in a family setting when arguments erupt, you will discover that Phlegmatic children try to negotiate and make everyone happy. If it doesn't work and the argument gets heated, you can see their eyes glaze over and a pasty little smile come to their faces. They may be looking at you, but "no one is home" . . . they tune out when conflict gets too heated.

If there is conflict in the classroom, Phlegmatic children won't even hear what's going on around them. They disappear into the world of their imaginations—a world that is peaceful. If your Phlegmatic child is struggling in the classroom, go check things out. You might ask to sit in the back of the room to observe the class and watch how your Phlegmatic child's behavior parrots the behavior of the other children. If they are in a classroom with an overbearing teacher, they probably won't perform as well as they would in a classroom with a nurturing teacher who can work with their strengths.

Phlegmatics enjoy doing homework with their friends or having their parents test them. They will excel in classes where they feel the teacher likes and values them; they may be unable to perform if they feel devalued by their teacher or peers.

Yes, my sweet Jeff is a Phlegmatic. He was a great baby! He smiled for the boss, giggled often, and enjoyed life. Then came school; it used to embarrass me to tell his teachers what I do for a living. Most of what I know about learning came from him, not from my classes.

He also has a visual/perceptual problem that intensifies under stress. It followed him all his life. In high school he struggled in both algebra and geometry. In Algebra I, Jeff would complete his homework. I hired a tutor who was a math teacher. The tutor verified that he understood the content, but he failed the test. I visited with his teacher after struggling with it on my own for a while. We brought in Jeff's test he had just failed, and I said, "Jeff, work this problem on the board." I told him to start with the last problem and then discovered he'd gotten it right. The teacher was surprised. He said, "That's the one most of the students miss." We discovered that Jeff had missed the first few problems on his test; they were the easier problems. (This often points to test anxiety.)

I showed the teacher that Jeff understood the content and asked, "How can we help Jeff?" The teacher's response was, "Well, I coach. Kids hit in practice, and strike out during the game. What can I tell you? Maybe he needs to go ahead and repeat Algebra I."

Jeff never thrived under his teaching; but because we knew he understood the content (verified by the tutor), I had him enroll in geometry. The details are different, but the outcome was the same: he understood content, verified by his math teacher and tutor. He got low test grades.

In Algebra II, we started the year with the same pattern—he did his homework; I checked it; he understood; I had him tutored; the tutor verified he understood content thoroughly; he did poorly on the first test. When I spoke with his teacher, he said, "I don't want Jeff to drop this class; he needs it! I can help him."

Jeff was able to conquer his test anxiety (an outgrowth of the time when his eyes were not tracking as they should); he earned a high B in Algebra II because one teacher said "I want to help him" rather than "Maybe he should try again next year."

Phlegmatics must feel valued at a personal level to thrive.

Jeff scored so high in math on his college entrance exams that he was not even required to take math in college. Make sure you know they understand the content, but cheer them on; always "vote for them."

Personality is need-based. Phlegmatics "need" to know the whole picture. Phlegmatics "need" relationships. Phlegmatics "need" peace. When their needs are met, they can understand detail and accomplish their life goals.

How to Spur Your Phlegmatic Children to Action

Listen. Spend some time sitting down beside them and listening to their day's experiences before you have them do homework.

Give think time. Have them draw a picture or write out what they are thinking before they jump into their homework. Phlegmatics need time to think. Phlegmatics, in fact, are embarrassed if they give an answer and the entire class laughs at them or even with them. They do have a great sense of humor, but their sense of humor is a dry wit. It is never acceptable to them to laugh at the expense of another. Before they begin their homework session, have them process what they are supposed to do by talking, writing, or drawing a picture.

Manage emotions. If they are frustrated over something that happened in school, have them do a "three-minute splash down" before they begin homework. Spend three minutes splashing down their thoughts, writing everything that they are frustrated about. When they are finished, have them look at what they have written and say, *"I won't let you get to me—I'm letting you go!"* They can tear up the paper. With your supervision they can burn the paper as they, symbolically, let their fear, anger, and/or frustration go.

Set time limits. Set a timer and give them a reward if they reach a milestone by the time the timer goes off. For example, give them five minutes to write a response to question number one or five minutes to work the first five math problems. At the end of five minutes, reward them for finishing what they set out to do (but don't punish them if they don't make it).

Work beside them. Sit down beside them with some work that you are doing, or have friends or brothers and sisters sit beside them and do their homework at the table. Phlegmatics are social beings and enjoy being part of a group, even when they are listening rather than talking. They learn a lot through listening and the feeling of camaraderie that comes from having other people sitting beside them doing work. Feelings of belonging help the Phlegmatic focus.

Depersonalize conflict. When Phlegmatics feel attacked on a personal level, they shut down emotionally and can't complete their homework. If they are frustrated over something, or if they are angry or upset, have them write out what's bothering them. The two of you discuss it, then ceremoniously toss it out. If they are too young to write, they can draw it.

Of course, every person is unique. It is important to treat your child the way he or she needs to be treated, building on strengths rather than harping on weaknesses. A strength carried to excess is what makes a weakness. For example, their ability to see divergent viewpoints, a great strength, carried to excess becomes the weakness of indecision.

Criticizing weaknesses—"Get your head out of the clouds"—lowers self-esteem and causes children to become weaker.

Praising strengths—"You're my sweet dreamer. I hope all your dreams come true"—builds self-esteem and empowers children to overcome their own weaknesses.

·················· **REFLECTION** ··················

In a workshop with children, I asked the question, "What would I have to do to earn an 'A' in your class if you were my teacher?"

The Phlegmatics responded, "You would have to connect with me at a personal level." The other personalities quickly shot back, "What does that have to do with 90 percent or better?"

Phlegmatics will never value accomplishment over relationship. If you have a Phlegmatic child, spend time listening to him. Spend time playing with her. It doesn't matter what you do. Phlegmatics don't need to be entertained; they need to be valued. They won't ask you to go to their school plays or ball games, but they will be hurt if you don't.

7

He Can't Sit Still Long Enough to Study

"He just drives me crazy! I start him on an assignment; then when I leave, thinking he's finishing his work, I find him wandering around the house talking to someone or playing a game. He doesn't understand why I'm upset—doesn't even seem to know he's doing anything wrong! He's fun, and I love him dearly . . . but I don't know if he'll ever amount to anything, he's just so wiggly!"

Who ever invented the "sit still and listen" classroom anyway? Let's take a look at the marvelous personality behind this common complaint.

The Sanguine Personality: Process-Oriented

About 38 percent of our children resent structure and need spontaneity and interactivity in their lives. They are social butterflies, flitting from one project to another, rarely finishing anything, and easily bored. They were wonderful babies. They probably enjoyed going places and meeting people. They charmed your friends by smiling at just the right times. Shopping with them brought you all kinds of interesting adventures; they never met a stranger. In fact, you thought they were perfect—until they started school.

Sitting still to learn is not their idea of a good way to spend a day. They have trouble completing assignments. This is not because they are being stubborn or because they are incapable of deep learning. Rather, it is because they live in the present—they really do forget to bring books home. You may have been called in for conferences with teachers because these children wandered around the room and didn't pay attention when the teacher was talking. Their performance may vary dramatically from one teacher to another because they react to the way they are received. Their performance may depend on the level of enthusiasm a teacher can generate.

Sanguines like fun in everything they do. If the teacher doesn't provide it, they create it—often to the teacher's chagrin.

 You thought they were perfect—until they started school.

Sanguines Live in the Now

When a Sanguine student is in class, that student is there 150 percent. When they leave the classroom, they are 150 percent gone. They literally can't remember when they stand in front of their lockers that they even have homework, let alone what it was and what books they need to bring home to make it happen. For this reason, you need to ensure that your Sanguine student keeps a master assignment sheet (see Chapter 13) and writes everything down. The last thing they do before they leave school is to check that assignment sheet so they know what books to bring home.

Sanguines Like to Talk

Our Sanguine children think with their mouths open. Much of what comes out of their mouths doesn't make a lot of sense and doesn't pertain to what they need to do. Because they talk so much and have seemingly disconnected thoughts, we have a tendency to discount what they say or to try to quiet them. In reality, these are the students who need to talk through an assignment before they sit down to do it. They actually "think with their mouths open."

If your Sanguine children are having trouble sitting down and doing homework, let them get up for a few minutes and move around. As they move, talk their assignments through with them: "Tell me what your homework is about," "Tell me about what you are going to say on this paper;" "Tell me how you go about doing this math problem." After they have had a chance to verbalize, they are ready to begin. The light goes on, and they have a handle on what they are supposed to do. Then you say to them, "Wow! It looks like you need to sit down and write that out really fast, before you forget it." The process of talking energizes them, and the process of standing up while they talk energizes them. Once they are energized, they can sit down and focus on their assignments.

When you sit down with Phlegmatic students, you very softly help them get through what they wanted to say. A Sanguine child, on the other hand, can follow you around the kitchen while you cook dinner and talk while you are working. Because Sanguines are good at multitasking, they can do several things at once.

Sanguines Are People Pleasers

Often with the Sanguine personality, we get angry with them for talking without thinking. We say, "I don't want to hear any more. Just be quiet, sit down, and get it done." When we understand the Sanguine personality, we realize that this is the wrong approach. It's like saying, "It's not okay to be you. Why aren't you someone else?" To carry it a bit further, it's like saying, "I always liked your Phlegmatic brother the best."

Since Sanguines are people pleasers, if we let them ramble in front of their peers, their peers will ask them questions they can't answer. When that happens, they are embarrassed. Peer pressure will cause them to work twice as hard next time. Sanguines work very hard to look spontaneous.

Sanguines do not respond to negativity or to correction; they respond to praise. Rather than pointing out their errors or telling them what they are doing wrong, describe what they need to do or how they need to think in order to complete an assignment. Catch them doing what they do well and praise them, and they will do better the next time.

These children respond to mnemonic devices (see Chapter 11), singing their assignments, marching as they study, and rewards (in fact, we often pay therapists to do this for us!). Punishment, however, rarely works.

Sanguines See the Practical Application

A Sanguine student can read a paper and not even know there are names, dates, and places in the articles they read. They may not even see the nuances of a relationship the way your Phlegmatic children will. But a Sanguine child will see the best and easiest way to do something. Sanguine children may struggle in the classroom, but as adults they will go out to do a job and do it well. Often they make more money than any of the other personalities combined because they are naturally gifted in practical applications. Unfortunately, practical application is not taught well in public schools (for example, being able to negotiate in a time of crisis is a practical application skill; being able to memorize names and dates of well-known negotiators is what's usually taught).

Because they have such vivid imaginations and are divergent thinkers, they go off in random and abstract directions in their thinking. If you have a Sanguine child whose teacher doesn't know how to respond to her, you will need to intervene for the sake of your daughter's self-esteem.

Sanguines Value Creativity

Sanguines are highly creative children. They love to play roles; they love to think up new ideas. They love to find new ways to try something. Because so few teachers know how to teach to and value this personality in the classroom, Sanguine children sometimes run into problems in the classroom where their creativity is not appreciated.

I once worked on a research paper with my nephew, J.R., a Sanguine fourth grader. He had done the research. Sanguine children enjoy research while they are learning something new. It's a little like finding a puzzle piece.

The paper was to be a factual research paper, and he had chosen to write it on Thomas Alva Edison. He would look at one of his note cards and begin with what he had written in his research brief. Because of his creative imagination, he would then create fiction that related to the fact he had just cited. The first few times he did it, I stopped him after he had finished his digression and said, "Let's look at the note card. The card reads . . . . You said . . . . You can see that you have created information that isn't there. That means you added things that aren't facts. I love your imagination, but your teacher wants a factual research paper, so for this assignment we have to delete your fiction."

He understood that. We removed it, but every few sentences he would launch into fiction again. After he understood the concept, when he would begin creating something fictitious about Thomas Alva Edison, I would stop the typing I was doing for him and start to giggle. He would laugh and say, "Oh, I'm doing it again, aren't I?"

Some would call this "abnormal" behavior. I call it Sanguine. As they mature, we need to teach these children to compensate for these needs, but we should never try to make them become someone they're not . . . and their creativity will serve them well all their lives. Teach them to manage it, but never stifle it.

We did get through that research report. I laughingly admit that he and I earned a C on it. It was four pages long, it had no grammatical errors, it had no spelling errors, it had flow . . . it had all kinds of good things. But he failed to bring me a copy of the teacher's directions and follow them. She was Choleric (see Chapter 9). She expected her directions to be followed exactly. He did it his way, and we earned a C.

How to Help Sanguine Children Achieve

Give accolades. Validate their creativity. Before process-oriented children can settle down to complete homework, their spontaneity and creativity need to be validated. Too often, we say, "Just sit down and be quiet and get busy." They come up fighting. Often, if they comply, the work they produce is of poor quality. When they feel good about themselves and are challenged, they are capable of great work. Building on their strengths, we might talk an assignment through with them. Then say, *"You have great ideas. Get them in writing fast before you forget."*

Set time limits. Set a timer. Tell Sanguine students exactly how much time they have to work on an assignment, and then set a kitchen timer so they can watch it tick off. This is especially effective for Sanguine children when they don't like the assignment, when it seems boring to them, or when they don't think they can do it. With a timer, they know that freedom is at the end of the few minutes; they just have to go through the motions.

Reward them often. If they finish with a minimum number of errors, find a way to reward them. The best rewards vary from child to child. For some, it is a ten-minute phone call; for others, it is playing a game with you.

Participate. Work with them. Sanguine children love interaction, so make a game of their homework.

Praise them. Praise their honest efforts. Sanguine children desperately need praise, perhaps more than any other personality type. Catch them in what they do well and validate them for that.

Communicate with teachers. In primary grades, you may have to maintain communication with the teacher to get accurate homework assignments. About the only thing that works to help them remember to bring work home is giving up recess if their work isn't finished. Generating excitement in what they're learning helps them to do the work. They respond to games.

As they mature, teach them to compensate for their needs. They might take creative notes in class to help them focus (see Chapter 14). They should be encouraged to study with friends—they learn best by talking! And by the way, don't stifle their creative imagination in the process of ordering their lives.

A strength carried to excess is what makes a weakness. For example, their ability to generate enthusiasm and live for the moment, a great strength, carried to excess makes people see them as shallow, a great weakness. Reminding them of their weaknesses—"You didn't really think that through, did you?" makes them weaker.

Praising strengths—"You're so creative. You'll think up something that will change the world some day"—builds self-esteem and empowers children to overcome their own weaknesses.

························ **REFLECTION** ····················

The Sanguine response to my question, "If all your teachers were like you, what would you have to do to earn an A?" was rather lengthy. They described enthusiasm . . . putting something extra into the class . . . showing you care.

I paraphrased, "So to earn an A in your class, you would have to do extra credit. Is that fair?" I meant "Is that a fair paraphrase of what you said?" They responded, "No. That's not a fair thing to do."

I asked, then, for a summary. They said, "We don't like having to do extra credit, but *you* would have to work that hard and do extra credit to earn an A if I was the teacher!"

8

He Spends Hours on Homework

"He does beautiful work, but it takes him hours. He's never satisfied, and he must ask me a million questions about everything. I'm glad he takes pride in his work, but there never seems to be time for anything else. Is that normal?"

Our sweet and sensitive scholars! These children work hard for good grades and formal recognition. Let's look at their personality.

The Melancholy Personality: Detail-Oriented

About 38 percent of all children need structure, order, and detail in their lives. They are the babies who cried when wet and were cranky if not fed on schedule. They may have been challenging babies, but they are wonderful students.

When they start school, our Melancholy children work meticulously on every project, and often don't feel their work is good enough to hand in. They may spend hours each evening on homework, never quite satisfied with what they achieve.

In one class, a group of Melancholy students told me that they are motivated by a pat on the back. This was an "aha" moment for me because their work is always beautiful. I didn't know that they don't know it is until someone else tells them.

In some ways, this personality is the easiest to help with schoolwork, because they are motivated to complete assignments and to do them well—even if it takes all night. However, perfectionism is not without its price. These children are often prone to depression because they can't quite achieve to their high inner standards. They mourn their errors!

Melancholies Zoom into the Facts

They naturally see the tree and the cell rather than the forest. They often need help discovering overall themes and how the details fit into the big picture of a subject. If they have teachers who move too quickly or teach application or concepts at the expense of detail and accuracy, they will become frustrated. If Melancholy children don't know exactly how the teacher wants an assignment completed, they will be frustrated. They are meticulous in following directions. When directions aren't there, their needs are not met, and they don't know where to begin.

Melancholies Need Validation

Before detail-oriented children can be comfortable handing in an assignment that doesn't meet their standards, they must have their desire for perfection validated. A comment such as, "That's good enough! Everything doesn't have to be perfect" points out their negative trait. Constant reminders of their weaknesses lower their self-esteem and disempower them from functioning in other ways. Instead, you might say, "You do such beautiful work; I'm glad you take pride in it. I'll bet your teacher didn't know how long this assignment would take, though. Let's quit for now, and I'll write her a note telling her how long and hard you worked on it." They won't like not being able to finish an assignment, but we parents need to balance their drive for perfectionism with our responsibility to protect them.

Melancholies Respond Well to Schedules

At the office one day we were discussing personalities, and we began to pick on the Melancholies (in a good-natured way, of course). We taunted them that they weren't spontaneous. Don quickly countered, "That's not true. I'm spontaneous. I schedule an hour every afternoon for spontaneity with my family!"

Many Melancholy students cannot function without lists and schedules. However, we learn more efficiently if we build breaks into our schedule, study dissimilar subjects in sequence, and study details in short spurts. Help them build a break into their schedules. That gives them permission to play.

Melancholies Need Some Alone Time

Most Melancholies are introverts. The primary difference between an introvert and an extrovert is where they get their energy. An introvert gains energy alone and spends it in a crowd. An extrovert gains energy in a crowd and spends energy alone. Since Melancholies are primarily introverts, this means they are full of energy and ready for class to begin in the morning and exhausted when they come home at night. The level of stress they have had during the day will match their level of exhaustion when they get home.

When they come home from school, they need your hugs. After that, they need some alone time. They definitely need a nutritious snack and some time to think, plan, and rekindle their spirits. When they are rejuvenated, they are ready to begin homework.

Because of their sensitive nature, Melancholies may be afraid to talk a problem over with you. They need you to sit down with them and listen to the details of their day: what they learned; how they are dealing with their peers, their frustrations, and their joys. Once they have been heard, they will be more able to tackle their task of homework.

Melancholies May Need Help Prioritizing

Often Melancholy children have a passion for art or music. They are also disciplined enough to practice, which means they develop their talent. When schoolwork takes them away from the hours they need to spend practicing, they may become depressed; they *need* to perfect their passion. You may need to monitor the time they spend on schoolwork and ensure that their inner needs are also being met.

 They are also disciplined enough to practice, which means they develop their talent.

When he was a senior in high school, my Melancholy nephew Eric became withdrawn. At all family gatherings, he was in his room doing homework. We watched his personality change. Music is his life; he could practice eight hours a day. Because he is also a disciplined student, he was in honors classes. His senior year he was scheduled for so many advanced placement classes that he didn't have time to pursue his first love, music. He was beyond the level of his high school band, and he was taking academic courses so advanced that he could use them as college core courses rather than high school electives.

He enrolled concurrently in his neighboring community college (half of his classes were for high school graduation; half were for college credit) which meant that he could join the community college jazz band and drop two high school courses. Because he was able to incorporate music back into his academic-heavy curriculum, in a short time, he was back to being our Eric!

How to Help Melancholy Children

Communicate with the teacher. Your Melancholy children will work hard to follow a teacher's direction rather than question an assignment. They tend to be shy, especially if their teacher is extroverted. They, especially, may need your assistance as they negotiate classroom procedures.

When I interviewed counselors to develop SCORE, I asked what they thought of my students' parents. The common response was "Those parents just don't care." They were armed with powerful ammunition: "We call home; they don't call back.

We hold events; they don't come. We send home failure notices; they don't even bother to call."

A friend of mine suggests that when we get more sophisticated with science, we will be able to prove through research that it is biologically impossible for a parent not to care. In the meantime, we must learn a lesson from these comments. Schools work harder when parents are visible! Make sure, when they see you coming, that people on campus can greet you by name!

 Schools work harder when parents are visible!

Listen. Take some time, when your children come home from school, to sit down and quietly discuss their day. Melancholy students tend to be soft-spoken; they don't demand your attention as some other children do. Melancholies will not respond to following you around the kitchen to talk. They need you—they need your undivided time. They feel unloved if you try to listen or talk on the run.

Schedule. Allow Melancholies to set their own schedule. You might tell them they need to be finished in 20 minutes, or dinner will be served in 20 minutes. When you set the timer for five minutes (as you would for your Sanguine children), it panics them because they can't imagine getting it finished in that short a time span. In reality, they probably can finish in that amount of time, but they stress over it when they have to. With my Melancholy students, I peek over their shoulders and validate what they have done; then I say, "Can you be finished in two minutes?" Usually they respond, "Give me three."

Praise. Praise them often and specifically. When you praise a Melancholy child, you praise a very specific piece of their work. For example, rather than saying "I liked your essay," you say "I loved the way you described the main character as pretentious."

Help them find what to do next. When your Melancholy son is frustrated with an assignment and feels as though he doesn't have what it takes to do it, he doesn't know where to begin.

Have him describe the assignment to you, and then tell him what you hear him say. Help him discover what to do first. Then you can say, "Great. Get that done, and I'll be back to help you in a few minutes."

Your Melancholy child will likely enjoy working alone. You just pop in and out to check on him every once in a while and sit down with him when he reaches the point of frustration.

A strength carried to excess is what makes a weakness. For example, Melancholies' attention to detail, a great strength, carried to excess becomes the weakness of rigidity. Harping at the weakness—"It doesn't have to be perfect. Hurry up!"— makes them weaker.

Praising strengths—"You pay such attention to the details. I can always count on you to do it right"—builds self-esteem and empowers our children to overcome their own weaknesses.

How Much Time Is Too Much Time?

According to "Helping Your Child with Homework" from the United States Department of Education, children in kindergarten through second grade average ten to twenty minutes of homework each school day.

Children in third through sixth grade average thirty to sixty minutes of homework each school day.

Homework at these ages should include reading—you reading to them, them reading aloud to you, and choral-reading a story or passage together.

Middle-school children might have thirty to forty-five minutes of homework per class per night, excluding lab classes and physical education.

High schoolers should have approximately one hour of homework per academic class per night.

College students will need to be self-motivated enough to spend two to three hours of study time for every hour spent in class.

If your child doesn't have homework, spend this amount of time in leisure reading to develop good habits (and to show the child who conveniently "forgets" to bring home his homework that forgetting doesn't add to play time). Once in a while, though, reward the whole family with a break.

If your children are exceeding these norms, discuss it with their teachers. Some personalities are more perfectionist than others; the teacher can let you know if your children are over-achievers and need to relax their standards. Other personalities daydream too much. Sometimes teachers have no real concept of how long an assignment will take. Your communication on these issues will help them make better judgments about what to assign.

When your child has labored over an assignment longer than is healthy, write the teacher a note about it to excuse your child from having to complete the assignment. When neither you nor your child can answer a question from the book's information, communicate that to the teacher.

Yes, as a parent, you have the right to question a teacher's assignment. Teachers don't know you have a problem until you talk with them.

················· **REFLECTION** ·················

You guessed it . . . to earn an A in a Melancholy's class, the students said you have to do the work and dig deep for meaning. You have to show you care. You have to study hard to master the details of the subject.

Would they take late work? "Of course! You can never get it finished on time if you do it right!"

9

She Does It Her Way . . . if She Wants To!

"She's very bright, but she's not very cooperative. If she wants to do an assignment, she does; if she doesn't, even God couldn't persuade her!"

These children will some day be our bosses. They'll be good ones if they pay the price of preparation. Let's examine their personality.

The Choleric Personality: Goal-Oriented

Approximately 12 percent of our children are goal-oriented Cholerics. They know where they want to go; they don't especially care for side trips. They are capable of doing great work, but it is work of their choosing. They may ignore the directions because theirs make more sense or because they don't respect the teacher. They feel they can teach the class better than the teacher, anyway. They fight to win—in fact, they enjoy a good battle, either with fists or with wits. As infants, when they cried you didn't just respond, you jumped into action!

 They are capable of doing great work, but it is work of their choosing.

They are seen as bossy children—they order the neighborhood around. Tactless as they appear, the other children follow their lead.

These children need control, power, and clear-cut assignments. Within those parameters, they perform well in the classroom. However, when they feel the teacher has given a vague, unfair, or unreasonable assignment, they argue about it. They may refuse to complete an assignment, or create their own guidelines.

Cholerics Are Self-Motivated

Cholerics are the only personality that doesn't need validation. They have an inner sense of motivation and an inner sense of right and wrong. This will be their greatest asset—and, at times, their greatest liability.

You can reason with Choleric children, even when they are young. I have had several Choleric children say, "I have the most awful teacher, and I hate him, and I am going to sit in his class and fail." As Cholerics they respond well to what we call "stinkin' thinkin'": "If you sit and fail the class, the teacher wins and you lose. You have to take the class again next year. That's 'stinkin' thinkin'. You want to win!"

Listen to your children until they begin to wind down. Then tell them, "You know, if what you tell me is true, I wouldn't like that teacher either. And, the way you describe him, it doesn't sound as though he likes you very much. But the teacher gets paid whether you pass or fail. He wins, and you lose. If you really want to get back at this guy, work like crazy and make him give you an 'A.' He'll hate it!" Our Choleric children, at an early age, understand stinkin' thinkin'. They may not yet understand that win-win is the only way to do life, but they do understand wanting to win. Even as small children, they can play the game of "working hard to get a good grade to drive the teacher crazy."

Cholerics See the Straightest Path

Because Cholerics are goal-oriented, they see the straightest path to a goal. This means they are frustrated when a teacher takes side trips. In classes where they have to go through the steps, such as proving a theory or working out a math problem, Cholerics can usually see the right answer. They don't see any reason to go through the steps. Their ability to see the straightest path to a goal must be validated. We need to explain to them that the first study skill is learning to read a teacher; you follow the teacher's directions in order to earn a higher grade. Cholerics, however, may choose to pay the price of a lower grade before they will comply with what they perceive as a "stupid" assignment.

Cholerics Need Their Intelligence Validated

Understanding this concept was an aha moment for me as a teacher. Cholerics always seem to have the right answer; they always seem to be in charge. When they are wrong, they are wrong at the top of their voice, and they believe what they are saying with a passion. For that reason, I was surprised to learn that in order to feel valued, they need to have their intelligence validated.

To you parents of a Choleric, that means when you are in conflict, you always need to let them know that you know they are smart. You always need to let them know that you know that their brain is working well. And, most often, they will respond to a logic-based argument. When you enter into an argument that implies "you're not very smart," Cholerics feel invalidated and unloved, and their performance begins to decline. We who watch often misread this decline in performance as "they just don't care."

Cholerics Need Help with Teamwork

Because Cholerics are not people pleasers, because Cholerics work well alone, because Cholerics take the shortest path to a goal, Cholerics don't necessarily do their best work as part of a team. They need help developing their social skills. Choleric children will go far in life, but until they learn to become a team player and to gather an appropriate support group around themselves, they will be stuck in entry-level positions. Because

Cholerics are goal-oriented, once they understand that compassion and teamwork are virtues, they set out to gain them very quickly.

If you have a different personality, it may be hard for you to give concrete directions. When you are communicating with a Choleric, they see your inability to give a clear-cut directive as a weakness. They don't respect someone who doesn't "shoot straight," or tell the truth. These children respond well to reasoning about the consequences of poorly prepared assignments. They also respond to competition and goal setting. Checklists work for them. They do not respond to compromises; they see people who compromise as weak.

Cholerics Need Control

Often when Cholerics are angry with a teacher, what is really going on is a power struggle in the classroom. They have a teacher who is strong enough not to give up power to them; and for a Choleric, not being in charge is frustrating. Once they learn how to work with the teacher rather than fighting for control, they work well. In some cases, that teacher ends up being their favorite.

I once worked with a family whose middle-school daughter was struggling. She had been placed in remedial classes. I looked over her tests to discover that her remedial placement was based on only one subset of the test because she did not know the definition of the term they used in the directions. When I gave her the definition, she rattled off the information correctly. Based on that, I empowered her parents to place her into college preparatory courses where she belonged.

I also discovered an interesting family dynamic. We looked at the personalities of the family: Mom was Phlegmatic. Daughter was Choleric. Mom had divorced when she was young, and Choleric daughter had been making most of the family decisions her entire life. Within a few months of them meeting with me, Mom married a wonderful man who was also Choleric. With Mom's remarriage, her daughter lost her position of power.

Fortunately, they got help, learned about meeting one another's real needs, and made some conscious decisions before too much animosity had developed. Once they understood that Cholerics need control, that Cholerics need to make their own decisions, and that as the father in the home, the new dad had the right to make some decisions for the family, they were able to negotiate what each one would control. They learned to appreciate and honor one another.

How to Help Choleric Children

Give them some control. Give them some power over their decisions. Personality is need-based. Choleric children who feel they are out of control will fight—you, the teacher, even the system. If they can't gain a sense of some control over their lives, they tune out and quit working altogether.

Help them with checklists. Help them make their own checklists. They work well from a list of their choosing, but not necessarily from one that is superimposed on them.

Let them move around. Remember that your Choleric children can multitask. Allow them to do two things at once as long as they meet their goals.

Teach tactful communication. Help them learn to communicate tactfully with their teachers. When they are frustrated, they have a tendency to fight rather than to reason.

Allow them to make and learn from poor decisions. The only ultimate failure is falling down one more time than you get up. Your Choleric children will learn as much from their failures as from their successes, and they have the courage to begin again. Help them through this process.

A strength carried to excess is what makes a weakness. For example, Cholerics' ability to make quick decisions, a great strength, carried to excess becomes the weakness of being overbearing. Criticizing their weaknesses—"Why do you always have to be right?"—causes them to become weaker.

Praising strengths—"You always seem to know what to do. Some day you'll be the big boss"—builds self-esteem and empowers children to overcome their own weaknesses.

······················ **REFLECTION** ·····················

What do you have to do to earn an A in a Choleric's class? The Choleric students in my workshop responded, "you have to do the assignment, following my directions." Would they take late papers? "Only with an advance doctor's excuse, and you would always lose partial credit."

Compassion is not their forte . . . but since they are goal-oriented, they develop it quickly when they learn it is a virtue.

10

The Dilemma of the Working Parent

"There is never enough time for homework, and she's always exhausted by the time I get home. For that matter, so am I. In today's world, parents work. How does anyone hold down a full-time job and keep up with their children's school work?"

It is amazing what we accomplish when we need to. Give yourself a pat on the back! It is difficult to be a parent, even if you don't work outside the home and even under the best of circumstances.

I am a working mother and raised Jeff as a single parent. When he attended daycare after school, we could rarely make it home before 6:30 P.M. He was always ravenous, so homework before dinner was futile. Because he played hard all day, he needed to be in bed by 9:00 P.M. Getting dinner, eating, doing homework, mothering, loving, bedtime chores, practicing music, devotions, leisure reading, Little League, church, and community activities were confined to two and a half hours each evening. Usually homework and music practicing were points of deep conflict between us.

Frankly, I resented spending the only time we had together doing tasks chosen by his teacher. I know that mothers are supposed to read to their children about one hour a day, but there was never an hour left after worksheets, spelling, math, and art projects. And I resented the fact that after completing these tasks, which he was too tired to do well, my final daily hours were spent doing dishes, picking up the house, and feeling guilty about my inability to find the time to make a living, love, nurture, and pass on my true values, both in words and in lifestyle.

Jeff usually had good—no, great—teachers. I am an educator; they were hand-selected. Yet he had busy work each evening, and much of this was his fault. He rarely managed to finish his work in the classroom because he was either daydreaming or socializing. As a result, he had far more nightly homework than any child should have to do. We who are blessed with those delightful Sanguine and Phlegmatic children have these issues to contend with every day!

Jeff also attended a great daycare center. They were supposed to supervise his homework and see that he had it done before I picked him up. But because he is innovative by nature (a great strength), he forgets what is out of sight (a corresponding weakness). The daycare attendant didn't question the fact that he rarely had homework, and certainly couldn't be expected to pick it up for him before they left school. When Jeff did bring homework to daycare, he learned that if he interrupted the other children often enough with his antics, he could be excused to the playground. Could you pass up such an opportunity at age five, or seven, or eleven?

My recommendations, in this chapter especially, come from years of deep frustration as a working parent, combined with my perspective as a professional educator. Your stories may be similar to mine; they may be dramatically different. But the following guidelines should be helpful.

Do Away with Guilt

"I just feel so guilty all the time; I am constantly torn between my needs and his. Always, after I have been away on a business trip,

I come home to a parent conference with his teacher. I keep thinking, "I'm supposed to be giving these things, not getting them!"

These words, from my journal, reflect my deep struggle to be both working mother and old-fashioned mother. I learned through counseling that part of his struggle was legitimate "separation anxiety." Another part of it was that he had learned how to press my guilt button. We had to cope with both.

 Admitting our guilt frees us to look at possibilities for a win-win resolution rather than wasting time justifying our actions or shutting down under the pressure.

There are two kinds of guilt: true guilt and false guilt. True guilt is guilt we deserve because of poor choices. False guilt is guilt we heap upon ourselves for being the way we are, or for circumstances in our lives over which we have no immediate control.

True guilt can be resolved by facing the truth, talking it out with one or more trusted friends, and changing the circumstances that bring it about. The process is simple and effective; it is at least as old as the Bible. Admitting our guilt frees us to look at possibilities for a win-win resolution rather than wasting time justifying our actions or shutting down under the pressure.

False guilt can be resolved only by changing you. It is a prime candidate for the serenity prayer: "God, grant me the serenity to accept the things I cannot change, the courage to change the things I can, and the wisdom to know the difference." Those who face severe struggles with guilt will benefit from counseling; often the root dates back to childhood. Twelve-step programs help us work through the issues that feed false guilt.

The only working parent who is dealing with true guilt over the issue of not being a full-time parent is the one who has chosen to work for economic gain, intentionally ignoring the needs of the children in the process. If you were that parent, you would not be reading this book.

Sometimes we work because working is easier than facing the problems we have at home. If this is you, run—don't walk—to the nearest source of help. Your children's futures depend on it. Data indicates that children of dysfunction (alcoholism, abuse, violence, etc.) will repeat that dysfunction in their own families. We *always* want more for our children than we have for ourselves. For our children to have a chance at life without our baggage, we must break our patterns of dysfunction and model healthy behavior.

Facts for Families

The American Academy of Child and Adolescent Psychiatry offers Web information entitled "Facts for Families." Their Web site will provide you with invaluable information on a variety of disorders that disrupt the flow of family. Visit *www.aacap.org* and click on "Facts for Families."

At times we confuse necessities with economic gain. If you struggle with guilt and have another source of income, consider changing your work situation. True guilt can find a win-win resolution through meditation, discussion with friends, and creative thinking. False guilt makes your situation seem hopeless.

Sometimes we struggle with guilt over balancing our personal needs with those of our children. Some parents need to work for personality and self-esteem reasons rather than economics. If you fall into this category, true guilt can be resolved by using part of your income to provide for your children's real needs (perhaps a nanny or a loving "grandmother") while you work to gain the energy to parent more effectively when you are home. Part-time work or work that can be accomplished in part at home might provide you with the ability to meet both your needs and those of your children. In our age of computers and modems, this is a viable option.

Sometimes we struggle with guilt because we haven't faced the facts. If we have no economic choice about whether or not we work, we must work. If we must work, guilt over leaving our children is counterproductive and robs us of the energy we need to utilize the time we have together. I have found that journaling about such frustrations helps me sort out my thinking and release my emotions.

Assess Your Situation

Much guilt centers around our inability to be Superparent. But then, that is an issue all its own.

I once heard news anchorwoman Rita Davenport comment, "Talk about guilt! Try being a home economics teacher who doesn't cook!" I was a home economics teacher, so my ears perked up. She went on to say, "I've found that my children don't know Oreos aren't homemade if I pop them in the oven first!"

A parent who works full-time cannot do everything. Look at all your circumstances and decide, based on both values and resources, what can be changed. Ask the following questions.

Are We Morning People or Evening People?
I am evening; my son is morning. We moved piano practice to before school and gave him responsibility for getting up earlier. When fresh, he accomplished more in less time.

What Are Our True Values?
If we believe quality time is more important than doing dishes, we may want to use paper plates or eat out more often.

What Is Important to Our Children?

Are Scouts, Little League, and music lessons attempts to fill voids from our own childhood or attempts to provide our children with socialization and self-esteem? Do our children benefit from them as much as we do?

What Other Issues Are Present?

The vicious cycle—not finishing work at school, forgetting to bring it to daycare, and not having any homework—may be your child's effort at control or at guilt, either consciously or subconsciously. Or it may be, instead, a classroom management issue.

What Options Do You Have?

Some things can wait until the weekend (or month's end?). Some can be dropped altogether. Some can be scheduled more effectively, such as eating before homework; a hungry child has an impaired short-term memory. Some chores can become the child's responsibility.

What Resources Do You Have?

Look to people! Two working parents can share responsibilities, trading off homework with meal preparation and dishes. Older brothers and sisters can tutor younger children. Perhaps a neighbor is in the same situation. Trading nights so one neighbor helps all children with homework while another cooks and does dishes is a great way to work smarter rather than harder. It will provide you with a little extra time and a lot of moral support!

I finally resolved part of my time issue by eating out more often (in cheap restaurants, of course). Thus, even though we arrived home later, we had been able to spend time talking about our day and relaxing a little before we faced homework. Jeff wasn't hungry when he started homework, so he was more productive. Time in both meal preparation and clean-up was saved. Of course, that meant guilt. I had to compromise my belief that meals in restaurants weren't as valuable as meals around a dinner table. In sharing my false guilt with a friend, she commented, "Your children will remember special times as those spent at home with friends; mine will remember them as times in restaurants. It really doesn't make any difference—they all will remember special times."

Loving, Not Homework, Is "Quality Time"

Jeff's story was the same every evening. He was supposed to bring his homework to daycare. He was supposed to *do* his homework at daycare. When I picked him up, we could have "quality time" together. The problem with this scenario was that he couldn't seem to remember to bring his homework to daycare . . . in fact, he couldn't even remember that he had homework until I picked him up and meddled in the matter. So during our "quality time," we would return to the school, seek out the custodian to open his classroom, secure his missing books and assignments, and spend our "not-so-quality time" doing homework.

Finally, the custodian, tired of having to walk across campus to open a door for me, told me I was a rotten mother because I should have my child home in bed, not at the school retrieving books. He implied that if I were a "good" mother, my son would remember his books. But what he jarred me into remembering was much more powerful: There is more to life than doing homework. Some of it is our responsibility. Sometimes we must give responsibility to our children, even if it means temporary failure. We can lose a battle in order to win the war.

I talked my situation over with his teacher. We dropped my "homework policeman" role and gave him responsibility—he would lose recess if his work was not done. Since recess was just about his favorite subject, he reluctantly complied (most of the time).

We must never get so caught up in the daily task of "doing" that we forget about our true values. Our normal children have all the brain capacity required to learn everything they need to know to function in our society. While it is important to help them progress steadily, the reality is that they can fill in their learning gaps and gain new knowledge and skills when they are adults.

 Sometimes we must give responsibility to our children, even if it means temporary failure. We can lose a battle in order to win the war.

If, however, we fail as parents to provide our children with love, hugs, affirmation, a sense of pride, a sense of worth, a system of values, approval, a sense of belonging, security, and a sense of competence, they will spend their entire adulthood seeking these things.

Never make your children do things (including homework) at the expense of letting them know they are persons of worth.

Give Your Child Responsibility

Jeff and I were discussing some of his childhood issues recently. He made a statement, and I commented, "I can tell you that I tried really hard over that one."

He laughed and responded, "Yeah, Mom. I have to hand it to you. You tried really hard with things where you had absolutely no control."

The organization ToughLove has a saying: "You can't control what your child does when out of your home." We must give our children responsibility for their own achievement (in bite-sized pieces, of course). We must allow our children to fail—and support them while they learn from their mistakes. We must teach them how to begin again.

When being the homework policeman is causing friction in your personal relationship, it may be time to throw the ball into the child's court. Although you need to encourage, support, and assist in the process, the ultimate responsibility for learning lies with your child. If homework has become a power struggle in your family, discuss it with both a counselor and the teacher. Then, perhaps, you should allow your child to face the consequences of missed work and a low grade. Keep in mind tht this should be done before they enter high school—otherwise their college admissions grade point average will suffer.

Remember, however, that a child who is truly struggling to understand content needs help, not responsibility. This tactic is only effective when strategically used on the underachieving child.

The nutshell guideline for making this decision is answering two questions:

- Can he do it himself?
- Should he do it himself?

If your answer to both of these questions is yes, it is time to forfeit your role as enforcer of good study habits. If your answer to either question is no, you are still needed in the equation.

Discuss Homework Options with School and Daycare

I still get queasy when I recall it. He was only in third grade, and I had to be at a 7:00 A.M. meeting. That meant leaving him all alone, standing in front of the school at 6:45 A.M.; he wasn't allowed to go on campus until 7:30.

I prayed a lot. In hindsight, I think I should have quit my job!

Because society is changing, schools are realizing their need to provide homework centers and tutorials within the school day or after school. Share your need to have homework done before you get home from work; ask for the help of your school. Suggest they seek help setting it up from SCORE—that's what we do!

Even if they refuse you, you will have planted a seed. Your problem can help someone else in years to come.

Discuss your unhappiness about daycare policies if they allow your child to play rather than do homework. After snacks and some play time, daycare centers should require all children to do homework for a period of time and have staff available to help. Those who conveniently have no homework should spend that time reading rather than playing or disturbing friends.

You have the right to expect—and the responsibility to insist on—cooperation and understanding in these matters from the school you support with tax or tuition dollars and the childcare agency or person you pay to represent you.

················· **REFLECTION** ·················

I struggled with guilt for years over not being able to serve milk and cookies, take nature hikes in the afternoon, and be the parent I always thought I "should" be. I prayed and felt guilty about it. I read books that implied that those who prayed could be gainfully employed in the home and still be a full-time mother, and felt guilty about it. I concluded that God must not think too much of me.

One year I took a full week off to work on a book I was writing. I was so depressed by Friday that I returned to work a day early. Finally it dawned on me that I am an extrovert; I need people! All those years I had received what I'd needed rather than what

I'd asked for. I fretted over my son's needs, but I certainly didn't know how to nurture myself!

Be gentle with yourself. If you are a working parent, you, too, have needs. You can "do" and "be" for your children only to the extent that you also take good care of you.

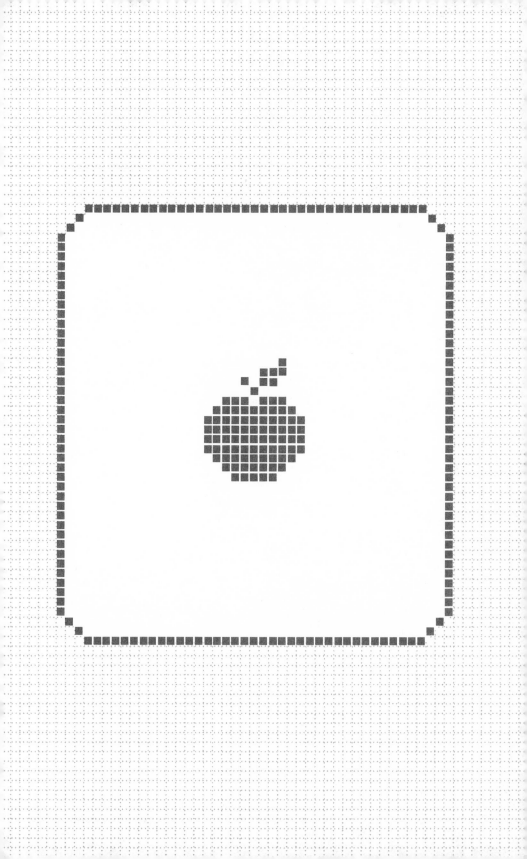

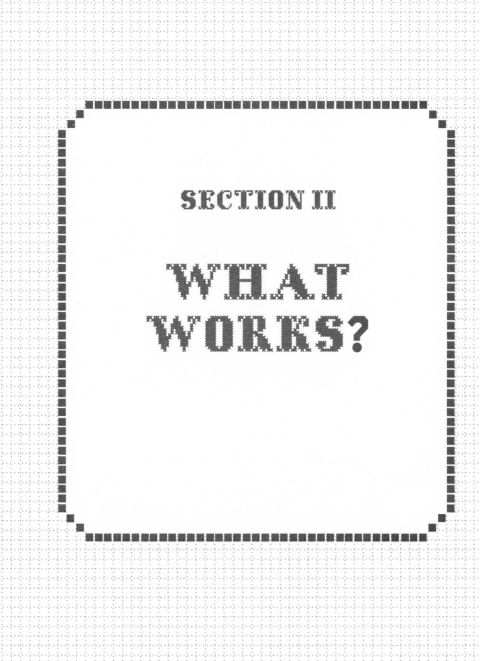

SECTION II

WHAT WORKS?

Jamie is an artist. He has that unique ability to look at something and make it prettier, cuter, more eye-appealing. When he listens to a teacher talk, he doesn't hear names, dates, and places; he sees images. His images convey the theme of literature, the meat of mathematics. His images do nothing to improve his GPA.

Susan has been dramatic all her life. She can memorize play lines and deliver them with an emotion that brings audiences to laughter and tears, that causes them to stand in applause. Susan can memorize entire plays, but she can't seem to remember her math facts.

Edward could be considered a "nerd." He can make computers do things most of us don't even know to try. Teachers can always count on him for a thorough but confusing answer. He carries on great conversations with adults but doesn't know how to talk with his peers.

These students are at risk of dropping out of school. Like their predecessors—Walt Disney, Lucille Ball, Albert Einstein, Thomas Edison—they are also "at promise" of genius.

 These students are at risk of dropping out of school. They are also "at promise" of genius.

Parenting: The Wonderful, Terrible Adventure

Parenting is tough.
We try to help our children learn, but they forget . . .
or fight us . . .
or try but don't succeed . . . . So
we feel insecure. We have done all we know to do. So
we wonder if *they* have a *problem*.
We hate ourselves for having those thoughts, so
we shove them into our subconscious where they
fester and periodically erupt!

During the eruptions, we seek help. We see
teachers,
friends,
doctors,
therapists.

We are rigorous in our pursuits, but often to no avail. So
we conclude that our children have an attitude problem and
need to take responsibility for their own learning. We worry
about the life lessons they will have to learn because of their
stubbornness, but what can we do? So we give up . . . until the
eruption occurs again.

We see
teachers,
friends,
doctors,
therapists.

We feel powerless. We are limited to what worked for us.
In many cases, we don't even understand that, and we are as
frustrated as our children.

When we use wrong approaches,
our children feel homework is punitive.
When we voice or show our frustrations,
our children sometimes use our insecurity to manipulate us.
When we imply they must not be trying,
we make them feel stupid.
This results in lowered self-esteem, which, in turn,
results in their further inability to learn.

It's time to break the cycle! A few tools and a little understanding can change the cycle of defeat. We have learned so
much about learning in the past ten years that you will enjoy
putting new theories into practice as much as your child will
enjoy success!

REFLECTION

I taught keyboarding back in the olden days when it was called typing. My first year of teaching, I discovered that if I didn't make students learn how to calculate margins and learn measurements, I'd spend the rest of the year correcting their errors.

My second year of teaching, I introduced the subject and said, "Now, take notes on this. You'll have to pass this test with a C or better in order to pass the class."

A young man six rows back on the center aisle yelled out, "Hey, teach, you don't know me. I don't do tests."

I responded, "In my class, you do. It's my job to teach you." When the lecture was over, I buzzed back to his desk and corrected his notes.

When I gave the first test, eight of the forty students earned either a D or an F. While the others were working, I gathered them together and said, "Evidently I didn't teach this the way you need to learn it. Let's review." I retaught the content in every way imaginable: mathematically, visually, by memory, measuring. Three students had to take the test three times, but everyone passed.

The next year, I began the same lesson: "Now, take notes on this. You'll have to pass this test with a C or better in order to pass the class."

A young man six rows back on the center aisle yelled out, "Hey, teach, you don't know me. I don't do tests."

Before I could respond, the student sitting across from him tapped him on the shoulder and said, "Hey, but in here she means it. You better take notes."

11

How to Help Your Children Memorize

"I'm worried about him. He studies for hours trying to memorize his vocabulary terms. I think he knows them, but he fails the test."

Take comfort. A lot of students fail tests on material they know. The reasons are myriad. Usually a few techniques will resolve the problem.

"I can never learn my times tables! Never!" he groaned.
Being a kind, compassionate, understanding mother, I responded, "Sit in this chair, and study, and don't get out of the chair until you know your times tables."
You know the voice of guilt—"Fine example you are! You teach teachers, and you can't even be kind to your own son." I returned to apologize. Then I experimented with the techniques I use in high school, wondering if they would work on such elementary learning as times tables. They do.

When you "work smart rather than hard," memory is easy! First, learn a few things about your child.

Logical or Spontaneous?

One of our most exciting new frontiers is brain research. It has far-reaching implications as we help our children learn. Daily we are making new discoveries about this incredible computer we wear on our shoulders. Our brain is far more marvelous than any machine.

The left lobe of our brain controls logical, orderly, sequential learning. It is the left lobe that stores most data and information. The right lobe of our brain controls spatial, relational, and interactive functions. Of course, barring brain damage, our entire brain is working all the time.

In years past, we called our learning either "left-brain dominant," meaning it focused on logic and acquisition of facts, or "right-brain dominant," meaning it focused on feelings, concepts, or relationships. Most of our teaching focused on left-brain activities. As a result, a right-brain-dominant student often had difficulty in school—not in learning, but in translating what was learned into typical vehicles for measuring what learning has just occurred. To a right-brain-dominant student, learning facts and data seems both boring and unimportant.

Because of computers, our children are growing up "duo-dominant," meaning they function equally well using logic or relationships. Our approaches to learning should also focus on the entire brain. If our children have difficulty understanding a concept, we can approach it through their right brain by converting it into a picture or by using a real object. In the movie *Stand and Deliver*, for example, fractions were taught by cutting up an apple.

The use of right-brain techniques has proven effective in reducing test anxiety for children. If students get nervous and can't remember information stored in their left lobe, use of a mnemonic device—a song, a game, their imaginations, or a picture—can serve as the trigger to reduce tension and access their memory bank.

Thinker or Experimenter?

Think for a moment of how you go about learning something new. Let's say you want to learn to ski. What will you do first?

Go skiing? Call a friend and ask how to ski? Buy a book and pick up pamphlets that tell you how to ski? Take a class, either on or off the slopes? Go shopping and buy a new outfit?

How would you plan a vacation? Let's say you have decided to tour New England this summer. Will you plan out every day, making hotel reservations long in advance? Read about every attraction, deciding ahead of time what you want to do? Talk to friends who have been there recently, asking what to see and do? Get your airline tickets, rent a car, and go spontaneously from one attraction to another, asking the locals what to do? Read a history book about the area?

Chances are you would combine some strategies, but most of us have a preference for how we acquire new information. If we have a *visual* preference, we will read or look at pictures to gather information. If we have an *auditory* preference, we will ask a friend or teacher how to do something. If we have a *tactile* preference, we will write about or build something in order to learn. If we have a *kinesthetic* preference, we will talk it through, usually while we move around. Often we will do something as we explain it, correcting ourselves in the process. We literally "think as we speak."

If your children are struggling to learn, watch them study. Discover their learning preferences.

Visual

If your children read quietly and understand what they read or if they quickly glance at pictures to gain understanding, they may be visual learners. They learn instinctively by seeing: reading; watching; examining charts, graphs, and projects. *If they struggle to understand*, have them convert words into pictures (or draw a picture for them) to help them comprehend.

Auditory

If your children mouth words, quietly reading aloud to themselves, they are probably auditory learners. This means they often need to hear something explained or read aloud before they feel confident about trying it. They may understand material, but perform poorly on a test. They often overlook little words, reading what they thought rather than what they saw. Sometimes this is accompanied by a mild visual disorder and can benefit from vision therapy (see Chapter 23). More often, however, it is their learning modality. *If they struggle to learn*, have them read aloud as they study and quietly mouth or whisper words when they take a test. Mouthing words will slow them down enough to catch the little words their eyes often overlook.

Tactile

If your children doodle or follow lines in a book with their fingers, they may be tactile learners. This means they learn best by touch. *When they struggle to learn*, have them write out or draw a picture of what they read. Have them take notes as they read. When they have their own books, have them use highlighters to mark key passages. Help them build models, talking as they work, to discover the full meaning of what they are striving to understand.

Kinesthetic

If your children can explain a concept or perform a task, but have trouble passing a test on the same material, they may be kinesthetic learners. Kinesthetic learners learn through processing, usually verbally, and often by talking their way through something. *If these children are struggling*, explain something and/or read aloud to them. Then have them re-explain it to you. Kinesthetic learners are active rather than passive. They may need to march, chant, or sing to acquire new information.

Work for Content Mastery

Which is the right way to learn?

Your children will likely tell you that visual learning is right because they have been chastised so often with the words,

"You didn't read the directions!" Actually, all are right ways to learn—or, rather, all are right ways to *begin* the learning process.

Content mastery comes from beginning at your point of strength and working through at least these four primary approaches to learning.

If your children don't understand what they read, read aloud to them as they follow along. If they still don't understand, have them write or draw a picture of what they just read or create a visual picture with them. If they still don't understand, you might act it out with them. Kinesthetic learners learn faster if they walk around the room while they read, perhaps to a rhythm.

Don't stop with these modalities! Brain research is opening up new avenues for acquisition of information every day. Look to music, sports, dance, reflection, discussion, and games for help. Learning *is* difficult; but at its best, it is a *passionate* difficult process that engages us at the core of our interest and value system. Tap into these core needs, and you won't be able to *stop* your children from studying! (That may not happen until they turn thirty-nine, but it *will* happen when they find their passion.)

Modality approaches to learning are for acquiring new information. Students haven't truly mastered material until they can understand what they read and know if it is right; can listen to someone explain or discuss it and know it is correct; can do it or write about it; and can explain it to another person. In other words, *content mastery* comes from beginning at your point of strength and working through at least these four primary approaches to learning.

Work with your children from their individual learning preference to acquire new material. Then practice or review from the other modalities.

Memory Tools for the Logical Learner

If your children are detailed and logical, they usually prefer a structured approach to memory. Try any combination of the following:

The Formula
Creatively combine the following learning theories:

- Repeat every item three times.
- Study in five- to fifteen-minute intervals.
- Review material anywhere between two and twenty-four hours after having studied it
- Use many senses to increase learning.
- Study fifteen to twenty-five items at a time.
- Study only what he or she doesn't know.

The Flash Cards
Flash cards are a great tool for memory. You can make your own by cutting 3" × 5" cards in half. Place the key word or symbol on one side and the item you wish to remember on the other. For example, to memorize math facts, 6 × 8 will go on one side, 48 on the other. To memorize vocabulary words, the word will go on one side, the definition on the other. To memorize a foreign language, the native language word will go on one side, the language translation on the other. In a law class, the case name can go on one side, details of the case on the other. Flash cards are especially effective because they can be rubber-banded together, carried, separated easily, and pulled out a few minutes at a time. You'll be amazed at all the times you can find five minutes. You know—the grocery line, the fast-food car line, the swim meet while waiting to perform, the doctor's waiting room, the restaurant waiting area. . . . You get the idea!

 You'll be amazed at all the times you can find five minutes.

The Process

Once the flash cards are prepared, work on fifteen to twenty-five items at a time. Set a timer for five, ten, or fifteen minutes. Mix the cards up. Have your child go through them one at a time, speaking the answer to the item out loud three times each, while looking at the question or key word. If your child is a tactile learner, have him write the item as he says it. If your child is a kinesthetic learner, have her march to a beat as she says each item. After repeating it three times, move the card to the bottom of the stack, and repeat the process with the next item:

Six times eight is forty-eight;
six times eight is forty-eight;
six times eight is forty-eight;
Nine times eight is seventy-two;
nine times eight is seventy-two;
nine times eight is seventy-two. . .

When the same card rotates to the top of the stack, repeat it three times again. Rotate through the cards for at least five and no more than fifteen minutes. Then set the cards aside.

The Review

Wait two hours, but no more than twenty-four hours, to review what your child has just learned. When your child reviews, shuffle together all flash cards. Divide them into two stacks: Those he knows, and those he needs to study. Have him spend the next five to fifteen minutes studying only what he doesn't know, in the same manner as before. For each review, rotate in a few new cards, keeping the study stack to between fifteen and twenty-five items.

In another two to twenty-four hours, he is ready for the next review. By this time, he will have learned some new facts but forgotten some old ones. Therefore, mix all cards together and divide them again. You will find that he learns new material, but forgets old material with each round.

"I'm amazed! I was sure when you gave us those words I'd never learn them, but I did!"

"Well, it did work, but it was so boring!"

These remarks came from teachers attending my study skills workshop. They had just learned to read shorthand using the above techniques. Read on for how to solve the problems of your children who are easily bored.

Memory Tools for the Abstract Learner

Flash cards, as described above, are a structured, rote activity. If your child is creative and can't sit still for too long at a time, you can add the following techniques to help with memory:

- Organize learning into categories.
- Associate it with something you know.
- Make an absurd association.

Categories

Have your children organize what they need to learn into categories. The typical categories are:

A, B, C, D . . .

A: Apple	B: Banana	C: Carrot

1, 2, 3 . . .

1. Read all chapter headings.
2. Read the questions at the end of the chapter.
3. Turn each heading into a question.
4. Read to answer the questions, etc.

Animal, Vegetable, Mineral

Animal	Vegetable	Mineral
Gecko	Peach	Rock
Horse	Carrot	Gold
etc.		

Time, Characters, Action

***Frog and Toad Are Friends* by Arnold Lobel**

Time	Characters	Action
First	Frog	Ran up the path
		Knocked on Toad's Door
		Shouted "Toad, Toad"
Second	Voice Inside	Said "Blah."
Third	Frog	Cried "Wake up!"
Fourth	Voice Inside	Said "I am not here." Etc.

Association

Help your child remember what he is learning by associating it with something known. For example, put new words to an old song. Children are much better at this than adults, and you will be amazed at how much information you can pile into the rhythm of a familiar song. See if you can sing a portion of the Gettysburg Address to the tune of *Twinkle, Twinkle Little Star*. Try it again to the tune of *Row, Row, Row Your Boat*:

Four score and seven years ago
Our fathers brought forth on this continent
A new nation, conceived in Liberty,
And dedicated to the proposition that all men
Are created equal.

Absurd Associations

Help your child create an absurd visual image for what he wishes to remember. The more absurd the association, the more likely they are to remember it. This can be accomplished by drawing pictures, creating cartoons, giving animate characteristics to inanimate objects, exaggerating proportions, or matching items to numbers and their rhyme word. For example, one group of students drew a Buddha waving an empty plate in the air. This helped them remember that Budapest is the capital of Hungary. Another group imagined a baby peacock, wearing glasses and waving a pointer toward the globe while adult peacocks watched in awe. This helped them remember the vocabulary word precocious (a play on the word peacock), which means maturing early. Another group, to remember the Spanish word *peso*, imagined a life-sized "piece of the rock," that is, money.

"Well, it worked, but it was such a waste of time! I could have memorized the entire list by the time we played those word games."

Another group of educators in the same workshop didn't relate to absurd visual images. They prefer formula memory techniques to those involving imagery. Everyone is different. We all need some structure; we all need some variety; we all need options.

It takes about the same amount of time to learn new items (approximately one per minute of study) by visual imagery as it does by rote memorization. Usually imagery is easier when a group of people combine their imaginations to create the visualization. I start children with rote memorization (sets of three, five to fifteen minutes, using all senses). We then switch to visual imagery when we get down to the last five to seven items that seem to be creating a mental block. Visual imagery actually serves as a right-brain trigger into the left-brain memory bank. It reduces test anxiety.

"You know when you taught the high-school students how to memorize the other night? Well, I've used it in my college classes, and it's amazing! Thank you."

Many such comments came from the college coeds who were tutoring high-school students at my church the week before finals. I spent just five minutes of the tutoring session teaching everyone these simple learning techniques.

Memorizing Paragraphs

Use the same theories a little differently to memorize paragraphs. You might, for example, write the work to be memorized on a chalkboard. Spend five to fifteen minutes in the following sequence:

1. Read the paragraph aloud three times.
2. Erase a word at random.
3. Read it again three times, filling in the blank aloud.
4. Erase another word at random.
5. Read it again three times, filling in the blanks.
6. Continue this process for at least five minutes. Then:
7. Copy the paragraph from the board, filling in the blanks (remember to check spelling if the test is to be written).
8. Leave it for two to twenty-four hours.
9. Repeat the process, picking up from where you left off.

"Would that work for play lines, too?"
(You guessed! A drama teacher in my workshop.)
"Yes, but have them walk as they memorize."
"You're right! They learn better when we walk in circles. Now I can add the sets of three and short time frames. They'll be on stage in no time."

Memorizing Play Lines

When trying to memorize lines to be recited, rather than written, use the same basic theories, but walk or stand as you might during delivery. Use rhythm and voice inflection as kinesthetic devices to help you remember. With the script in your hand, read a word or short phrase. Look away from the script and repeat that word or phrase three times, emphasizing a different word or syllable with each repetition. Look back to the script and repeat the first word or phrase, adding the next word or phrase to it. Look away from the script and repeat both phrases three times. Continue this process through one paragraph.

Start the process over with the second paragraph. When you have completed the second paragraph, say it three times added to the first paragraph. Continue this process, in segments of five to fifteen minutes every two to twenty-four hours until you know your part.

"It works! It really works! I taught my Biology students to use these techniques, and then I said, 'Promise me you won't study longer than five minutes!' Quiz grades went up in every class."

It is important to watch how your children respond to each approach to learning and work the way they need to learn. For example, my son found writing especially tedious. I worked with him verbally and visually, always seeking a way to motivate him to do written work. In seventh grade, we finally found the culprit: a slight visual disorder. Vision therapy helped resolve it. Using our computer helped us work around his apparent frustration with written work until we could discover what was wrong.

······· **REFLECTION** ·······

"First, you can learn your times tables. Remember last year when you passed your test on twos, threes, and fours? They're the same thing; they're just mixed up this year. You've already learned them."

(It's vital to point out past successes when our children are emotionally committed to failure).

"And secondly, you *will* learn them; you have no choice over that. The only choice you have is whether or not you will let me help you."

(When students know what to expect, they are likely to adjust their behavior to receive the reward and avoid the punishment).

First we divided the flash cards into two stacks: those he knew and those he needed to study. He already knew several, so watching the huge stack diminish began to build his confidence.

(Divide and conquer. Study only what you don't know.)

Knowing Jeff is an auditory and kinesthetic learner, I had him speak the problems out loud, three times each.

(Use many senses to increase learning.)

After modeling the process for him, I set the kitchen timer where he could see it tick off five minutes.

"And what do I have to do then?"

"Whatever you want. Your other work is done."

(Students need hope. Giving him a time frame significantly improved his attitude. I had just reduced his ninety-five-year sentence to the chair to just five minutes because he could "never learn his times tables—never!")

We mixed them up again the next morning, and Jeff repeated the process for a second five minutes. He passed his test that day.

Use these principles to empower your children to acquire information. But more importantly, use these techniques to stimulate your imagination to try something new.

12

How to Drill for a Spelling Test

"My daughter does all the spelling homework the teacher assigns, but she does poorly on her spelling tests. She slaughters spelling in her writing assignments, too. Is there hope for her? Is it true that some people just can't spell?"

Don't give up yet! Yes, some very bright people have trouble with spelling, but most students can pass their spelling tests with a few proven strategies.

The year I learned shorthand, my English teacher wouldn't let us erase, cross out, or write over on a spelling test. One week, on about word thirteen, I thought, "How do you write a chay?" Chay is a shorthand sound for the "ch" blend words, as in "change" and "watch." Shorthand is a phonetic alphabet. I had been using phonetic spelling with long-hand symbols on the entire test. It worked until I came across a sound that didn't have an English counterpart. Because of class rules (not an understanding of content), I failed the exam.

Usually spelling words come with a group of assignments that allow children to use the words in a sentence and write each one three times. However, most students also need someone to drill them after they have studied and before they take their test. Your children can study for a spelling test using some of the same techniques utilized for memory.

Auditory or Kinesthetic?

If your child is an auditory or kinesthetic learner, you can drill for spelling tests on the run. I used Thursday and Friday mornings, driving to school, for such tasks. You simply call out the word and allow the child to spell it for you. If it is correct, you affirm the answer and give the next word.

When a word is misspelled, you comment, "Not quite. Try again." If spelled correctly the next time, have them repeat the correct spelling three times (remember the theory: sets of three).

If they miss it the second time, you say, emphasizing the correction of their mistake, "No. Listen carefully. Affirm is spelled A-f-*f*-i-r-m. Now you try it." Again, if they spell it correctly, have them repeat it three times.

If they miss it again, say, "Let's try it together. You spell it with me." The two of you spell the word in unison: *"A-f-f-i-r-m. A-f-f-i-r-m.* Now you do it." Your voice through two trial runs gives them confidence and practice.

If they still miss the word, leave it until a later review. By this time, they are frustrated and have developed an anxiety over this particular word.

As you continue through the spelling list, review each word that was missed next time a word is missed. Affirm, for example, might have been word number four. Perhaps your child then missed word number nine. After studying nine, go back and review four, then go on to ten.

Visual or Tactile?

A parent in one of my workshops commented, "What do you think is going on with my daughter? I study with her, and she knows how to spell all the words. But when she takes the test, she misses four or five words. Why can't she remember?"

If your child is a visual or tactile learner, you need to drill for spelling tests while she is seated at a table so she can write.

Give her a word and have her write it. Peek over her shoulder with each word, to see if she spelled it correctly. If she misspelled it, tell her, "Not quite, try again." Repeat the entire process as much as you would for an auditory or kinesthetic child, but use writing rather than verbal clues.

As you help your daughter study for a spelling test, it is important that you check the words one at a time; don't go through an entire exam with a misspelled word. That way you work with her at the point of her error, and she has a vision of correct spelling in her mind before she moves on through the test.

If she tries for the third time and still misspells it, give her the correct spelling. Have her rewrite it the correct way three times.

But She Still Fails the Test

If your daughter knows all the words but misses several on the test, you need to affirm her intelligence. Children who study but fail a test feel stupid. You might comment, "But you knew those words. You spelled them for me. Something else must have happened when you took the test. We'll find the culprit! Tell me about the test." Often children don't know what happened, so you will have to lead with questions:

 You need to affirm her intelligence. Children who study but fail a test feel stupid.

How Did the Teacher Give the Test?

Did he use the words in a sentence? (You are seeking whether you studied rote memory but the teacher used context. If so, change the way you study.) Most teachers are testing for spelling within context because recent research suggests we learn to spell by reading good literature. This means that spelling tests may be dramatically different than they were when you were in school. It also means that your children might not even have spelling tests. Ask your child's teacher how to help.

Did You Forget During the Test but Remember after You Handed the Paper In?

(You are looking for test anxiety and/or some mild visual-perceptual problems.) If this is the case, use mnemonic devices as you study with your child. They serve as triggers into the memory. Try:

1. Marching or chanting while you study to involve movement and intonation.
2. Singing the spelling out as opposed to speaking it. Speaking is controlled in the left lobe of our brain, singing in the right.
3. Drawing a picture to create a visual image. Art creates a right-brain trigger.
4. Creating an absurd visual image of what you're trying to remember. This triggers our imaginations. We make a visual image absurd by exaggerating proportions or giving animate characteristics to inanimate objects, as in *Honey, I Shrunk the Kids*.
5. Creating a sentence out of the letters of the word. For example, using the word a-f-f-i-r-m, you might create a sentence such as "**A F**ine **F**riend **I**s **R**eally **M**ine"—A-F-F-I-R-M.

These triggers relieve test anxiety, allowing students to access their memory banks during a test. In the 2006 movie *Akeelah and the Bee*, Akeelah used the jump rope as a mnemonic device to trigger her memory and relieve test anxiety.

Mama tried to help me with my homework, and sometimes it got me into trouble. She always taught me silly ways to remember things . . . like Mississippi's capital is Jackson. She taught me about Mrs. Pie Pie and her son Jack. To remember Louisiana's capital, Baton Rouge, she taught me that Louisiana battled on the rouge. I got to school eager to recite this for my teacher. I guess she thought I was being smarty. For some reason, she didn't appreciate my sense of humor—or Mama's.

—From *100 Years of Memories!* A tribute to Fannie Scott's 100th birthday, as remembered by her son, "Junior."

Did the Teacher Pronounce Some of the Words Differently?

You are seeking classroom keys that may confuse the child, such as an accent or relationship with the teacher that might be distracting. If so, discuss it with the teacher or school counselor to find a joint resolution.

Did Anything Happen in Class that Distracted You?

You are seeking information about the "quiet/noise" process (see Chapter 2); was the test to soft background music, but your child needs quiet? If so, teach your children to compensate for the atmosphere not provided by the classroom to meet his own needs.

Perhaps you studied the words in order but the teacher mixed up the words on the test—they usually do! If so, study with the words mixed up.

Perhaps you studied, as described above, in an auditory and kinesthetic (hearing and speaking) manner, but your child is a tactile and visual (writing and seeing) learner. Quit studying in the car—give practice tests in writing. As they write, have them say each letter out loud. I don't believe a child should misspell a word and move on, however. This plants misinformation in the mind's eye; it is appropriate for writing fluency, but not for spelling tests. In your practice test, check every word immediately after it is written. If incorrect, immediately have them correct it and write it three times while spelling it aloud.

If a child spells it correctly aloud but misspells it in writing, look for a vision or hearing disorder (see Chapter 23). In your final review, have your child write the word while quietly mouthing the letters but not allowing any sound to come from his mouth.

Perhaps your child is kinesthetic and auditory, but the test was given in a visual, tactile manner. Once you realize this, teach your child to compensate for his auditory need by silently mouthing the letters as he writes them. This silent mouthing provides the benefit of another modality and often helps the kinesthetic learner sit still long enough to take the test. You can make a game of trying to read lips to show a young child how to mouth words silently.

Perhaps your child has test anxiety. If a cure isn't immediately found, discuss your tactics with the teacher. Training your child to breathe deeply, flex his shoulders, and use mnemonic devices helps. Sometimes a teacher will allow a child to be tested as part of a tutorial session in order to lessen anxiety and find out what is really remembered.

 When they have no knowledge base, learning to spell is meaningless.

Perhaps your child is right-brain dominant. Create acronyms and visual images to help him remember words.

Perhaps your child is both right-brain dominant and kinesthetic. Study and drill while marching to a beat.

Perhaps your child is an extreme goal-oriented or process-oriented personality plus a kinesthetic learner. Tape words to the bathroom mirror and have her study while combing hair and brushing teeth. These active children often learn while doing routine chores that would otherwise be boring.

As you work with your children in spelling, remember to check their comprehension by having them use the word in a sentence. Spelling can easily become a rote experience, especially for language minority students. When they have no knowledge base, learning to spell is meaningless.

It is important to have your child study spelling words for a short time every day in order to build confidence and place words in the long-term memory. Each day, new words will be learned and old words forgotten. Review these words within two to twenty-four hours of learning them.

If your child reaches eleventh grade and still spells poorly, buy a "misspellers dictionary" and a computer program with a spell checker. Develop their other talents.

Also, look at your child's relationship with the teacher. Phlegmatic children need to feel valued in order to learn their best. Sometimes just the feeling (even if not a reality) that the teacher doesn't like them will cause them to freeze during a test. Usually this issue is resolved simply by the teacher stating, "I enjoy having you in my class." It's amazing what affirmation will do!

If the problem remains, consult your pediatrician or a behavioral optometrist (see Chapter 23).

REFLECTION

Now let's revisit my spelling test when I was also taking shorthand. Two tragedies occurred in that scenario:

1. Even though I realized why I had failed the test, I didn't talk to the teacher. I didn't question class policy. I didn't, at the very least, explain why I had failed that spelling test. Empower your children. Role-play with them. Have them pretend they are their teacher; you be them, and explain to the teacher what has happened. This gives them the benefit of a rehearsal before they talk to a teacher.

2. The teacher didn't talk to me about it; she gave me the F I earned. Why should she have talked to me? Because it represented a major change in my behavior. I was a great speller. I always made As on my spelling tests. I won the spelling bee in junior high school. She had administered the spelling bee; she "graduated from eighth grade" with our class and moved to the high school. She knew I knew how to spell and should have talked to me about it . . . but, then, she had about 240 other students to look out for. My parents only had one, this time around.

13

How to Maintain an Assignment Sheet and Notebook

"My son is one of those creative types. He has a notebook, but it is so disorganized. He can never find a paper when he needs it, and sometimes he loses his homework before it's time to turn it in. Is there hope for him?"

Your creative son may some day be our boss. And even the most disorganized student can learn some creative organization strategies.

"It drives me crazy! I ask to see a paper, and she digs through her book that is stuffed with folded, messy papers, in no particular order. Sometimes she can find it; sometimes it is lost—and it's no wonder! How could anyone find anything when it's that disorderly? Besides the obvious, it breaks the spine of a book. Students should be taught to respect the school's property.

"Well, no more. I've had it. I've warned my students! No more books stuffed with paper. Next time I see one, I'll dump it all out in the trash can. In my class, they keep a notebook!"

Yes, the above statement is true. Peter, a friend and high school teacher, actually does that. The statement speaks to a mismatch of personalities, but the issue is real. Your Sanguine/ Phlegmatic children will need help in organizing a notebook; they are usually "stuffers." Often they are packrats, but they are so disorganized that they can't always find their treasure. We need to help them work around this problem. But first, let's hear from a parent about assignments:

He drives me crazy! He never has homework. I've talked to his teacher. He's so bright that sometimes he doesn't have homework. More often, though, he just forgets. I can't tell whether it's legitimate or whether it's on purpose! Either way, I never know how to help him or what to work on.

Whether the teacher requires it or not, have your child keep an assignment sheet to copy the assignments for daily homework. Have them include the page numbers and any special instructions (such as "Answer questions one through five," or "Answer odd-numbered questions only").

Whether the teacher requires it or not, have your child maintain a notebook, even in elementary grades. It will develop good habits, ensure that assignments are accurate and communicated to you, and increase retention (because what is written down has received the benefit of both visual and tactile attention).

Personality Differences

Before we look at how to help our children organize their notebooks, let's look at how personality differences affect the way that they remember assignments.

Sanguines Live in the Now

They get so excited about a project or event, they know they will never forget. They learn by talking, so when an assignment is explained, they don't *need* to write it down; they understand perfectly. But, alas, out of sight is out of mind, so once they leave the classroom, these energetic children are off to bigger and better things. They don't even remember they had an assignment until about five minutes before class starts the next day.

To those who watch, this is disgusting. They are so good under pressure that they can usually do their entire assignment in the five minutes they have left—*usually!* And, of course, once they learn that this works, they may learn to con their way through life.

So you, their parents, have to dance a jig between affirming their strengths of enthusiasm and spontaneity and helping them organize themselves before they get into advanced placement classes.

Phlegmatics Are Our Dreamers!

They sit in class trying to listen. Because they need the gestalt in order to learn, a simple statement causes their minds to spin off in a dozen directions. That sets their vivid imaginations reeling. Before they know it, class is over, and they didn't even *hear* the teacher assign the homework. They really didn't think they had anything to do tonight!

Phlegmatics also, somehow, miss the idea in class that homework is to be handed in. Until a teacher or parent helps them make that association, they don't realize that they haven't done something they should do. They do mature, but it's a learning process for them.

Melancholies Are Our Perfectionists

Your Melancholy children are a different breed altogether. They often do the homework but don't think it's good enough to hand in. If they don't know how to do every problem, they don't hand it in. If they're insecure about an answer they gave, they don't hand it in. You may find their notebooks organized well, but their work hasn't been turned in, so they get no class credit for it.

You will want to look over their papers when they finish their homework and compliment them on it (a specific compliment on something concrete, not a general statement of praise). Tell them you're eager to hear their teacher's comments because you know they'll be positive.

Cholerics Do It Their Way

Our Choleric children are intuitively organized. They probably have their homework, have handed it in, and have received a good grade—or they have chosen not to do it, because "it was a stupid assignment."

Yes, you need to help them! But help them compensate within the self-esteem power of their strengths, not by shaming them for their weaknesses.

Assignment Sheets

An assignment sheet should be on card stock or heavy paper. Let your children creatively color code and/or illustrate the assignment sheet to match the class, if they would like.

Divide the page into four columns: Date Assigned, Assignment, Due Date, Grade.

Assignment Sheet

Date Assigned	Assignment	Due Date	Grade
10/22	Book Report	11/7	B+
10/22	English Worksheet	10/23	A
10/22	Math Worksheet	10/23	+
10/23	Read pages 12-15,	10/24	
	History Book		
Etc.			

In elementary school, one assignment sheet at the front of the notebook is adequate. It is maintained for an entire quarter. As one page is used up, place another on top so the most recent assignments are seen first.

In middle and high school, one assignment sheet is needed for each class. It is the first page behind the notebook divider. Again, it is maintained for an entire quarter.

Calendars

In addition to the assignment sheet, a monthly calendar in the front of the notebook should record all assignments and projects by the date they are due. New months go on top so that current assignments are visible.

Calendar

Sunday	Monday	Tuesday	Wednesday	Thursday	Friday	Saturday
1	2 Music Lesson	3	4 Little League Practice	5 Science Project Due	6	7
8	9 Music Lesson	10	11 Little League Practice	12	13 Book Report Due	14
15	16 Music Lesson	17	18 Little League Practice	19	20	21
22	23 Music Lesson	24	25 Little League Game	26	27 Book Report Due	28
29	30 Music Lesson	31				

Notebooks

Notebook fads come and go almost as quickly as fashion does. Periodically it is a fad for students to use the little spiral-bound notebooks rather than three-ring binders. Periodically it is a fad for students to have a little folder in lieu of a notebook. Although it is important socially for students to follow the trends, there are distinct disadvantages to using something other than a three-ring binder.

Since social approval is important to children, they will likely want to follow the notebook fad. Rather than trying to force them into a three-ring binder if it's "not cool" to carry one, help them decide how their notebook strategy is working. They may go through a semester or year with another style, but you will help them with future decisions. Ask the following questions:

1. Are your notes and papers easy to organize?
2. Can you add pages?
3. Do you lose pages easily?
4. Do you sometimes forget to change folders?
5. Are you sometimes confused about which folder to bring to class?

Notebooks should be organized by class with early morning subjects in front. A divider page is needed for each subject. All class notes, reading notes, handouts, and worksheets should be placed in the appropriate section of the notebook, usually by reverse date, with the most recent assignment first. Extra blank paper should be at the end of each section.

Studying from Notes

As children reach the age where they take notes to study for tests, they need help learning to study from their notes. Teach them to use a highlighter: Use one color for headings, key points, and categories within their notes; use another color to highlight what they need to study. Nothing else should be highlighted.

When students begin college without practicing this skill, they highlight everything in the book. That makes the material unusable for review; nothing stands out. They work "hard" rather than "smart."

Using Post-it notes as dividers helps students organize their notes to study for comprehensive or open-notebook tests. Have them write the subject divisions on the sticky tab. Then, as they read test questions, they can automatically turn to the correct section rather than having to thumb through their notes to find the correct information.

If students used this technique for an open-notebook comprehensive (covering information from an entire semester) examination in United States History, their divisions might be: Pre-Revolution, The American Revolution, Colonization, The Constitution and Amendments, The Gold Rush, etc. Their notebooks will look like this:

PRE-REVOLUTION

REVOLUTION

COLONIZATION

CONSTITUTION

GOLD RUSH

Making Notebooks Interesting

Sanguines like color and fun. Let them be creative with pens, pictures, and games. They respond to rewards, but rarely to punishment. Reward them often. Help them dig out their wrinkled, folded papers each evening and place them in their notebooks. Discuss the logic behind your organization strategy—Sanguines won't pick it up by watching.

Phlegmatics respond to relationship. Sit down a few minutes each day and let them explain their notes and/or assignments to you. Be genuinely interested in what they have to say. Affirm their ability to get everything down on paper so creatively. Encourage them to write reflections on their assignment pages. Remind them to turn papers in to receive a homework grade.

Melancholies value detail, order, and neatness. They don't know it's good enough, though, until they hear it from someone else. Praise them for their ability to maintain such a beautiful, organized, easy-to-understand notebook. Allow them to experiment with color or pictures to reinforce concepts. Spend time listening to them, and encourage them often. Assure them that their work is good enough to share with a teacher or friend.

Cholerics, on the other hand, do their own thing. They value power. Allow them to control *how* they will organize their assignment sheet; don't give up your control about *whether* they do an assignment sheet (at least in primary grades; they'll assume control of their lives soon enough!). Cholerics need their intelligence valued in order to feel loved. Compliment them on the thinking that goes on behind their assignment sheets and organization skills.

·············· **REFLECTION** ··············

When I started the SCORE program, I inherited the 600 students in ninth grade who were struggling in their classes. They were capable, but they were earning low grades. I interviewed them and got some interesting responses, especially about homework.

I expected to find that they had not done their homework. Instead, I found thick notebooks full of work they had done but not turned in. When I asked them why, their responses fell into 3 categories.

1. "I didn't think it was good enough." That speaks to the need for validation. Our children desperately need a pat on the back. I didn't realize that as a teacher. I thought they knew when their work was good, but most of them didn't know until I told them.
2. "I didn't know how to do number four, and the teacher doesn't let us hand it in unless we do everything." It never occurred to them to come early and ask a teacher, to leave a blank for number four and fill it in before class started, to call a friend, or to go to the library and get help from the librarian before school started the next morning. They just didn't hand it in and took their F.
3. And, of course, there is the classic response, "Was I supposed to hand that in? I didn't know I was supposed to hand that in." Remind your children . . . hand it in!

14

How to Take Notes

"I was never good at taking notes. I don't have a clue how to help my son. His teachers make a big deal of it, but is it really necessary?"

Yes, more teachers are demanding that students take notes than when we went to school. I'm teaching them to require it. Students who take notes retain more information. Read on!

A teacher who attended my workshop said I made such a big deal over note-taking that she decided to experiment. She didn't believe it would make much difference. She went back to her class and gave them a pretest. Then she had the students number off one, two, one, two, one, two. She instructed the ones to listen attentively while she gave a lecture and the twos to take notes. When she gave the post test, she became a believer. The students who took notes improved 38 percent more than the non-note-takers.

Why Take Notes?

More important than how to take notes is whether to take notes. The answer is yes. Every day in every class, take notes. Even in kindergarten.

Why? The reasons are myriad:

- Retention will triple, even if you never look at your notes again. You have heard material, written material, and seen material by taking notes. ("More senses—more learning").
- You have to actively participate in class if you are to take notes because you must shorten what is said into its essence—what is meant. You can't take notes without thinking.
- Taking notes will help to make a boring class more interesting.
- Taking notes will help you be more organized.

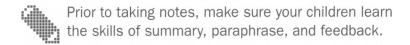 Prior to taking notes, make sure your children learn the skills of summary, paraphrase, and feedback.

Before Taking Notes . . .

So often we tell our children or students to take notes . . . then wonder why they don't. It's because they can't take notes until they have learned some communication skills. If they don't know how to block out distracting thoughts, they won't be able to focus and listen in class as they should. If they don't know how to listen for key words, they can't write fast enough to take notes. If they don't know how to interact with content, their minds pull them away. If they don't know how to question what they don't understand, their notes will be incomplete or inaccurate.

Prior to taking notes, make sure your children learn the skills of summary, paraphrase, and feedback.

Listening
As we work with students, we find their distracting thoughts often prevent them from listening in class. Too often, we say things like, "What's wrong with you? Pay attention!"

Actually, we should be saying, "What's right with you? Your brain is working!" We don't know quite how to measure thoughts, but we know we can think of many things while we read or listen to someone speak. We can read, if we develop our speed-reading skill, thousands of words per minute. We believe our thoughts can reach beyond 2,000 thoughts a minute.

If that is true, we cannot "pay attention in class" without thinking of anything else. With that in mind, we need to teach our children to manage their thoughts. My favorite strategies are:

1. Tell them it's okay to "go on vacation" in class. When they have been on vacation and come back, raise their hands. This humorous approach makes them aware of how often their thoughts carry them away.
2. Take class notes using two sheets of paper: one for class notes, one for notes to yourself. When the distracting thoughts come, jot them down. That way, you are free to listen without having to worry about whether you will forget. We have discovered that the same five to seven concerns can distract students thousands of times each class period.
3. Use double-entry class notes. In one column, write class notes; in the other, write your thoughts and reactions related to the notes.

Summarizing

Before your children can take notes, they need to learn how to condense material—how to shorten what is said or read. This skill is easier to learn from written material because they have the benefit of rereading if necessary. They must develop this skill by the time they reach high school so they can listen to between 120 and 200 words per minute and condense them into approximately twenty words that represent the key points of what a teacher is saying.

Summarizing is a skill that has to be retaught at various developmental levels. Elementary children are concrete thinkers. Somewhere between elementary and high school, they learn to think abstractly. As their thinking changes, they need to relearn, experience, and practice various skills.

Practice summarizing with young children by having them retell stories you read to them (this can be done as soon as your child can talk). Encourage them to ask questions and imagine endings to stories as you read them.

I teach middle- and high-school students how to summarize by having them cross out all the words in a sentence that aren't necessary to the meaning. For example, let's look at one of SCORE's Learning Theories:

A student will learn material more thoroughly if asked to explain it to someone else.

Although summarizing is highly personal (meaning that there is more than one right answer), the key words in this sentence are **learn, more,** and **explain it**.

Paraphrasing

Another skill to prepare your children for taking notes is the ability to paraphrase—to say the same thing in a different way, to find the overall meaning in a literary work, and/or to apply a concept in a new setting. Using the same theory *(A student will learn material more thoroughly if asked to explain it to someone else,* or *learn, more, explain it),* a paraphrase might be "Sometimes you learn by talking." Small children might practice this skill by seeing how many words they can think of for the same thing: Fido, pet, dog, fleabag, good boy.

When your children begin telling you a story that matches the theme of the story you've just read them, they're actually practicing the skill of paraphrase. Encourage them to do that. It's a great skill and will serve them well all their lives, but often it isn't valued in the classroom after our children leave elementary school.

Another form of paraphrase is the one-sentence theme. In one sentence or less, what was the whole story, or movie, or lecture about? As you watch a movie, sing a new song, or read a story, you can make a family game of coming up with the most creative one-sentence paraphrase.

The County Superintendent of Schools once accompanied me on a visit to a high school SCORE class. Toward the end of our visit, last year's class heard we were there so twelve students dropped by to meet us. I said to them, "Dr. Dean doesn't really know what SCORE is. Tell him in one sentence or less." Without hesitation, they went around the circle. Everyone gave a different one-sentence paraphrase, and I couldn't have said it better:

SCORE teaches you to build a plan to reach your dreams.

SCORE helps you master coursework by helping you to think differently.

SCORE shows you how to make decisions that move you toward your goals.

SCORE teaches you good study skills.

I said, "Tell Dr. Dean what you want to do." Again, without hesitation, each student recited a career goal.

Dr. Dean quickly responded, "And how are you doing as you prepare?" Around the circle they went again, without hesitation: "I have a 3.6 GPA." "My GPA was 3.8 last year; it's dropped to 3.7 this year." "I had a 3.2 last year, and I'm earning a 3.6 this year." Then we reached a young man who said, "I've really blown it this year. Last year I had a 3.2. This year I've gotten into sports and let my grades drop. I have a 1.8."

I didn't need to say anything because the students all jumped him: "Yeah, and you're making us look really bad. You better get your act together!"

Feedback

Feedback is the art of clarifying information to make sure that the student understood what the teacher intended to say. Simply stated, when a teacher says something and the student doesn't understand it, the student asks questions. Help your children create thoughtful questions to ask in class the next day. Teachers think students who ask questions are trying harder. Because of that, they treat these students differently; they begin to anticipate their questions and coach them in their understanding. They use these students' questions in class discussion to clarify information for other students. In short, asking effective questions brings benefits to everyone in the classroom. This skill will serve them well throughout their lives.

Teachers think students who ask questions are trying harder. Because of that, they treat these students differently.

Remind them that they are to ask real questions, not those meant to distract. Distracting or "smart aleck" questions will result in receiving special attention of the wrong kind.

Help them create interesting questions, and check their understanding the next day to see if they got their questions answered.

As children mature, these feedback skills become much more sophisticated than is indicated by this cursory introduction. When a student gets angry at a teacher, the student tends to either "act out" or "wall off." We train our middle- and high-school students to use the skill of feedback to monitor themselves when they get angry at a teacher. They are instructed to "build a bridge back to learning, not a wall, and not a war." To do this, they are to ask non-offensive questions, ask for clarification, or put their confusion and/or their assumptions into words and ask the teacher for clarification. It will benefit your children tremendously if you help them think of appropriate, deep, and non-offensive questions to ask in the classroom.

To teach this skill to a group of Native American students, I insulted them. I stated, "When Columbus discovered America, he found a group of savages already living here that they called 'Indians.'" I then instructed them to build a bridge by using feedback skills.

Of course, they were incensed. I told them most of the time teachers don't mean to make you angry, and most of the time, because they "wall off," the teacher doesn't even know they're angry. In their small groups, they figured out how to "build a bridge."

One group asked a question: "How could a country be discovered that already had a people living here?" This is a great question! Non-offensive, and it causes me to rethink my statement.

 Feedback describes; it doesn't judge. Judgment has a winner and a loser; feedback makes sure you both win.

Another group gave me new information: "How could a people be called savage when they had already developed a written alphabet?" Great! It caused me to rethink my statement and realize I had chosen a poor term.

A third group went for body language and assumptions. As I made the statement, I was holding one of their children and making fun baby faces. They said, "What you said to us sounded racist, but it's obvious from the way you treated our child you don't feel that way. I don't think we heard what you meant to say." Wow! That one had me searching for a way to affirm—rather than insult—these bright and eager students.

Yet another student responded spontaneously. He said, "But I'm Indian." Had he stopped there, he would have had me. He couldn't do it. He added, emphatically, "Would you call me a savage?" I told him with the first statement he gave great feedback. I felt terrible for having said something that hurt him at such a personal level. With the second, however, he twisted the knife and started a war. I had to fight back.

Feedback describes; it doesn't judge. Judgment has a winner and a loser; feedback makes sure you both win.

Around developmental age ten and eleven, the brain begins to change in the way it acquires new information. Researchers such as Daniel G. Amen, MD, call that process fine-tuning the brain. In teacher terms, that means that our children, somewhere between sixth grade and high school, change from being concrete thinkers to becoming more abstract thinkers. They make new connections to seemingly unrelated things. They begin the process of changing from being a generalist to being a specialist. Thus, even though they may have learned communication skills in primary and elementary grades, they need to be retaught and fine-tuned as the brain changes and they begin to think differently.

Note-Taking Strategies Using Pictures

Younger children, right-brain dominant learners, children who have trouble sitting still, and children who are not fluent in English may have great difficulty with traditional notes. These children succeed with a "concept map." A concept map uses words, pictures, and symbols. The dominant idea is placed in the center of the page. Each sub-topic is clustered around the topic, forming a circle around the main idea. The cluster includes words, symbols, and pictures that form a visual image of key ideas. A different color may be used for each subtopic.

The concept map may be highly artistic; it may be quite plain. Concept maps should have the class, date, and topic included in the central idea. They can contain a great deal of detail.

The moment children pick up pen and crayon, they can make a concept map. Read them a story and ask them to draw it for you.

On the following page is a concept map on communication skills: Summary, Paraphrase, and Feedback.

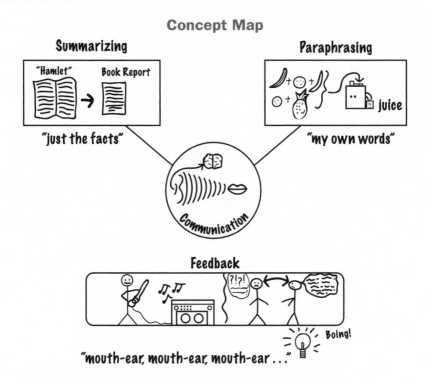

Concept Map

Note-Taking Techniques Using Language

As your children learn to read and write, they take notes using language. Have them make a wide left margin on a sheet of notebook paper. Notes are to be taken in the right column and only on one side of the paper.

In the upper right-hand corner of each page, the class, topic or page numbers, and date should appear. Some teachers will request additional information in these spaces.

Ask your child to summarize by writing down the important things the teacher says in the space on the right. Add the skills of paraphrasing and offering feedback when your child is ready. Notes should be taken in the style that is most comfortable and natural to your child. If your child thinks in a language other than that of the classroom, notes may be taken in the dominant language. Otherwise, content is lost because of the effort to translate.

Common formats include complete sentences, outlines, and topical indentations. Examples of each follow, using the paragraph on summarizing and using the combined techniques of summarizing and paraphrasing.

Complete Sentence Notes

To summarize what someone says:
- Shorten what is said or read.
- Write only key points.
- Have them retell stories to you. Encourage asking questions.
- Imagine new endings to sentences. Cross off unnecessary words

To paraphrase material you read or heard:

Outline Notes

I. To summarize what someone says:
   A. Shorten what is said or read.
   B. Write only key points.
   C. Have them retell stories to you.
      1. Encourage asking questions.
      2. Imagine new endings to sentences.
      3. Cross off unnecessary words.

II. To paraphrase material you read or heard:

Topical Indentation Notes

Summary:
   Shorter
   Key Words
   Retell Stories
      Questions
      New Endings
      X-off extra words

Paraphrase:

When your child begins homework each evening, sit beside him to discuss and review class notes. A review within twenty-four hours helps move the content from short-term memory into long-term memory. It gives you an opportunity to help with the communication skills necessary to taking effective notes. More importantly, however, it helps you spend a few minutes sitting beside your child. Your presence in his life activities sends a positive message of his worth.

Remember to compliment your child about something related to the notes before offering suggestions, and remember that notes are personal. Your child may not say things in writing just the way you would. Notes are acceptable if your child knows what they mean well enough to explain it to you, and if the content is accurate. Explaining notes to you also reinforces learning—remember, we learn 95 percent of what we teach to someone else.

In the wide left margin of the paper, have your child predict a test question, write a key word, or draw a symbol for each major concept.

Many college professors now post their lecture materials online. College students download them and use their slides as an outline for taking class notes on their laptop computers. As you are teaching your children good skills for taking and using notes, make sure they also get into a good keyboarding class to prepare them for this natural next step in their educational careers.

REFLECTION

Now back to the real world. Did this work for me as a parent? The answer is that it was a lot more work for me than for him. Jeff fought me over this issue tooth and toenail. I developed a policy that the first thing he had to do when we got home was show me his class notes. When he forgot to take notes (legitimately or on

Test Question

Name three ways to summarize	To summarize what someone says:
	Shorten what is said or read.
	Write only key points.
	Have them retell stories to you. Encourage asking questions. Imagine new endings to sentences. Cross off unnecessary words.
	To paraphrase material you read or heard:

Key Word

Summary	To summarize what someone says:
	Shorten what is said or read.
	Write only key points.
	Have them retell stories to you. Encourage asking questions. Imagine new endings to sentences. Cross off unnecessary words.
	To paraphrase material you read or heard:

Key Symbol

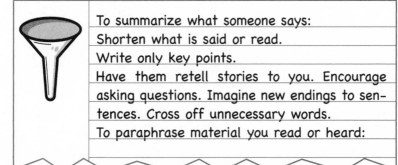

	To summarize what someone says:
	Shorten what is said or read.
	Write only key points.
	Have them retell stories to you. Encourage asking questions. Imagine new endings to sentences. Cross off unnecessary words.
	To paraphrase material you read or heard:

purpose), his first homework assignment of the evening was to re-create class notes from memory for every class. Eventually (very eventually with the Sanguine/Phlegmatic personality!) he learned it saved time to just get it done in class.

I stuck with it because I know it works.

By the time he got to college, he could take pretty good notes without my nagging. Our ultimate job as parents is to empower our children to be responsible adults. A friend of mine says, "If we do our job well, they leave home . . . and we cry."

15

How to Improve Reading Comprehension

"My daughter can read something perfectly, but not remember what she read ten minutes later. Are there things I can do to help her?"

Yes, there are many strategies to improve comprehension. Some of them are actually fun!

Mr. Jones worked in a tutorial setting with Ana. Ana was a struggling reader, and she was especially frightened of the timed reading tests because she could never finish the passage in the time allotted. Mr. Jones worked with her to build her speed. When she took her national test that year, she came running in, so excited. She said, "Mr. Jones! Mr. Jones! I finished the test this time! I looked at it, and I was so afraid, and I thought I could never finish reading it, and then I thought, Mr. Jones said, 'Read faster, read faster,' so I did what you said, and I finished the test."

Many years ago, in his book *The New Hide and Seek: Building Self-Esteem in Your Child*, child psychologist Dr. James Dobson advised parents to hire a tutor if their children were below grade level in reading at the end of first grade. He gave this excellent advice because he understood that a child behind in reading in first grade would likely never catch up in school. Children who are behind in reading in first grade are usually underplaced in math in seventh grade. This results in their inability to gain admission to the college of their choice; to enter most colleges now, students must complete Algebra I, Algebra II, and Geometry in high school.

I reiterate what Dr. Dobson says. If they're not reading at grade level, hire a tutor. But also have their eyes and ears checked.

The major academic focus from kindergarten through grade six is reading. Read, read, read . . . read some more . . . read everything. Have your children read to you. Read to them. Model reading. If you notice that your child is struggling with reading, in addition to hiring a tutor, discuss your concerns with your pediatrician (see Chapter 23). This skill is so key that if they don't master reading early, it will affect them for the rest of their lives.

In school, primary students "learn to read." Upper elementary-, middle- and high-school students "read to learn."

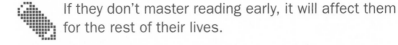

If they don't master reading early, it will affect them for the rest of their lives.

Automaticity

Have your children strive for automaticity when they're reading. Automaticity means that they don't have to decode words; they are intuitively decoding as they read. The process of decoding a word detracts from comprehension.

Look at the word comprehension and break it down into small pieces:

com – pre – hen – sion

If your children have to decode that word (break it into syllables or sound out each letter for pronunciation and comprehension), their energy is spent decoding rather than comprehending. Your children who read very slowly, obviously sounding out words, are not at automaticity in their reading yet.

Choral-read fifteen minutes a day, every day with your child. Choral reading means that the two of you read the same thing simultaneously, aloud. Read at a comfortable, slow pace, ensuring that your child can see the word as she hears it. If you do nothing more than choral-read, every day, fifteen minutes a day, you will see a noticeable difference in both speed and comprehension within one month.

This concept is so powerful that in our special programs, we require parents to commit to choral reading with their children. Choral reading becomes part of their homework routine each evening.

Learning to Read

From the moment he said his first word, it was obvious that Jeff would master language. He talked early; he talked often; he learned new words. When friends would visit, he would listen to our adult conversations and ask questions. As a toddler, he would often repeat the words he didn't know: "Fireplace. I don't know fireplace. What's fireplace?" "Orchestra. I don't know orchestra. What's orchestra?"

This ability to pick up on language would serve him well all his life. It would also, at times, provide us with embarrassing moments.

From at least the time of birth, our brains have an amazing capacity for language. Take advantage of this time in your children's lives. Talk to them about anything and everything. Use little words they can understand; use big words so they learn to ask the meaning and to predict meaning from context.

Take them to the library and have them select a book to borrow. As soon as they begin to read books, get them their own library card (all they need is your co-signature).

Children in kindergarten through the first half of second grade learn to read using three primary skills: phonemic awareness, phonics, and sight words.

Phonemic Awareness

Phonemic awareness is a pre-reading skill. It involves teaching our children to hear and say a variety of sounds. If you sing the "A, B, C, D, E, F, G . . . " song, you are developing phonemic awareness: the ability to distinguish letter sounds. If you read children's books to your preschoolers, they probably have begun to develop their "phonemic awareness" skills.

One phonemic awareness skill is the ability to distinguish between words that rhyme but create different sounds by changing only the first letter: fun, bun, gun, run, pun, sun. See how many words you and your children can create together, working through the alphabet for beginning sounds. Those silly rhyming books and fun books of children's poetry develop phonemic awareness. When you have a contest with your children to see who can come up with the most words that sound alike, you are developing this pre-reading skill.

As children develop, they learn to hear and distinguish these sounds. They then learn to tell where the sounds occur. For example, in the rhyme words above, the first letter of every word is different. In the list *bun, bus, bug, but*, all words start the same but have a different last letter, or "phoneme," or sound.

Phonemic awareness is an oral skill. Young children begin looking at picture books, pointing to a picture, and calling out the name: cat, hat, bat. Until these oral skills are developed, children cannot be expected to learn to distinguish written letters and relate them to sounds. Until they master sounds, they cannot blend them to make words.

Rhythm and music also help children with phonemic awareness. When they learn to clap or move to a beat, they are developing their ability to hear syllables. Playing games where they clap, dance, jump, hop, walk, or sway to a syllable is a good reading-readiness strategy.

Phonemic awareness begins at birth and increases steadily as they learn to talk. By the end of kindergarten, your child needs to be able to recognize, understand, and speak all basic sounds.

Phonics

Phonics is one of several reading and word-attack skills. Phonics is a great reading skill. If it were the only reading skill we need, it would be spelled "fonex."

Phonics teaches children to recognize the letters that represent the sounds that they learned using phonemic awareness skills, to combine those letters to make up words, and to write the words. As children develop phonemic awareness skills, they begin to read and reproduce the letters that form the sounds.

You can help your children by singing the alphabet song while looking at the letters rather than singing it from memory or while looking at pictures. Show your children a letter and have them tell you what it is and what sound it makes. First go in order (A, B, C), then show them random letters. When they have mastered letter recognition, you will be able to point to a letter at random and have them tell you its name and what sound it represents. Usually you begin with capital letters, then move to small letters.

As parents, you can help your children by looking at the individual letters and saying the sound repeatedly, perhaps using rhythm or song. Consonants are easier than vowels:

L, Sing L with me. L, L, L; L, L, L.

F, Sing F with me. F, F, F; F, F, F.

P, Sing P with me. P, P, P; P, P, P.

Now, let's sing them together: L, L, L, F, F, F, P, P, P.

You can have a contest to see how many words they can think of that have the P sound: peanut, popcorn, push, purple.

Then move the sound around: How many words can you think of that end with a P sound? Peep, keep, deep, weep.

Now put P in the middle, too: pepper, dipper, skipper, flipper, puppy.

Next we learn to use short vowel sounds:

A as in apple.

Then we can put words together:

P + A + L. Put them together (blend the sounds to form the word from the combined letters) and you have PAL.

As they progress, they learn more complicated sounds such as C, which can sound both like K and like S. Then they can put together C + A + T to form CAT. They learn about blended sounds: br, bl, sn, etc. They can practice the same way as above—singing or chanting the sound repeatedly, then adding a vowel sound, then adding a beginning and an ending: sn-a-p.

They progress from recognizing these simple words to reading words with two syllables: "tomcat."

As soon as they pick up a pencil or crayon, children can begin copying letters and drawing pictures of words.

By the end of second grade, your children should be able to read common words at automaticity, sounding out only unfamiliar words. If they are not at this stage, get them help. Reading is crucial to everything else they will do in life.

Sight Words

Children also need to develop their word recognition skills so they can read words like "phonics" without having to try to sound them out. To say that all children need is phonics is like saying "Lettuce is a healthful food. From now on, that's all you can eat."

Sight words are those that don't follow the rules of sound, such as the, was, they, of. Sight words are also those that appear in print so often that students need to know them by sight rather than sounding them out each time, such as but and that.

As they develop their sight-word skills, children learn to recognize common whole words. They can, for instance, read "the" rather than having to sound it out as "t-h-e: the." They learn to adjust their decoding skills to allow for unusual sound and letter combinations such as "ph" sounding like "f," and "g" sometimes sounding like "j," as in "change."

As children learn to look at words and sentences as a whole, their learning is enriched when they draw a picture of what they read, retell a story in their own words, create a new story from the ideas they just read, predict endings, create new endings, and write their own stories from the wealth of their imaginations.

Your child's teacher can provide you with a list of the grade-level sight words they will be learning each year. Your child should recognize all grade-appropriate words by the end of each school year. Most sight words are taught in first, second, and third grade; but complex sight words will be taught through grade six. If your child is not confidently reading grade-level materials by the end of each year, get help. All good learn-to-read programs have always taught a spectrum of reading readiness and word-attack skills.

 If your child is not confidently reading grade-level materials by the end of each year, get help.

Steps to Comprehension

As parents, our most fun task in helping our children learn to read is that of providing them with a wealth of experiences.

I work with high-risk youth. I will never forget the look of exhilaration on the faces of teens more streetwise than I will ever be as they saw the ocean for the first time—the looks of delight as their toes touched the sand—their absolute fascination with salt water waves.

I once gave a workshop for teachers who each brought a few struggling sixth- or seventh-grade students with them. For lunch, they visited a fast-food restaurant. These high-risk children didn't know how to order from the menu board. When the order-takers asked if they wanted to "super-size," they didn't know what that meant.

Reading comprehension is difficult to develop. This is partly because comprehension relies on a knowledge base, and every child's knowledge base is different; it is based on personal life experiences, perceptions, informal and formal learning.

Make sure your children have a wealth of experiences. Their brains constantly create and make connections from the known to the unknown to gain understanding. The first time Sandra saw snow, for example, she said, "Look at all that shampoo!" We teachers call that "scaffolding." To read, we must take advantage of prior knowledge. Shampoo was the only white, bubbly substance she knew, so when she saw a "white and bubbly" field of snow, her brain searched for something familiar to give her meaning. When children read about someone walking in the sand, it is difficult to imagine what that means unless they have felt their feet sink in the tiny grains while trying to walk or watched the granules sift between their fingers.

I have precious memories of Jeff's early life experiences:

The high school band marched along our street in practice. Every day we watched and marched along with them, beating our make-believe drums and playing our imaginary horns. When he was tiny, I carried him out. As soon as he could walk, we marched together.

As soon as he could sit well enough to don a helmet, manage the child seat, and ride on the back of my bike, we were off. I took him to a nearby ice cream parlor and bought him a soft-serve cone. I forgot, however, to bring him a change of clothes. We were both a bit sticky by the time we got back home.

Then there was the time he fed the ducks so enthusiastically that he fell in the duck pond along with the bread. That was another time I forgot to bring a change of clothes. Another experience. Another cause for laughter. Another precious memory.

I remember the first time his children's choir sang. He was three; the song was over by the time he finished finding familiar faces in the audience and waving to them.

And who can forget four-year-old soccer? He and another little boy fought over the only girl on the team while the game went on around them.

I didn't know it then, but all these experiences would serve him well when he began to read. They added to his knowledge base, giving him valuable scaffolding for future learning

Provide your children with a wealth of experiences. Experiences are free; the world around you is full of them.

 Developing comprehension is difficult because the writer, student, and teacher all have different knowledge bases.

Even before they can talk, help your children to think about making choices: "Do you want peaches or applesauce for dinner tonight?" As they grow, they can choose: "Do you want your milk in the green glass or the yellow glass?"

If they reach middle school and don't know how to order from a menu or the meaning of common terms for choices such as "super size," I promise you they will have difficulty reading and be labeled "high-risk."

Developing comprehension is difficult because the writer, student, and teacher all have different knowledge bases. Sometimes teachers teach children to explore their own imaginations. Then they give the required district or textbook tests where the author asks for a specific answer. Comprehension, then, also involves the ability to discern. We work from three perspectives:

1. Teaching the child to understand what has been said or read;
2. Teaching the child to realize that her understanding is not necessarily wrong if it is different from another person's opinion because there are various viewpoints; and
3. Teaching the child to realize that objective tests are based on what either the author or teacher think. In other words, to "play the game of education," it will be important for your child to learn to think the way the test-writer thinks. The first study skill is learning to "read" a teacher.

Birth

We know that children are born with some memory of what was said by those nearby during at least the last trimester of pregnancy. They are capable at birth of recognizing the voices of both their mother and their father. If reading comprehension is based on knowledge, this has far-reaching implications. Of course, their sense of security and love is far more important than knowledge. I wouldn't suggest reading Shakespeare aloud those last three months, although some future parents are doing it, based on this research. I would suggest, however, that comprehension begins by being read to and shown pictures from the time of birth. Keep lots of books around. Read to your children daily. Use a variety of words in conversation. They are developing their vocabulary as they listen. But, of course, you know that. It doesn't take them long to say words we wish they wouldn't.

Talking

When your children learn to talk, continue to read to them and have them retell the stories in their own words. Encourage their efforts. Cheer for their creativity. Read a story to them. Have them draw a picture or act out what you just read. Make sure you read a variety of books so they develop a broad knowledge base.

Growing

In elementary grades, children need to be able to understand what was read, predict what might happen next, and relate it to their life experiences.

As your children develop their verbal skills, read a story to them and have them make up another story of their own that is like the one you read.

Read a paragraph and ask them what they think will happen next.

When you read a story, help them remember the time they had a similar experience.

As they develop their motor skills, write the story they tell you on a large sheet of paper. When it is finished, cut it into puzzle pieces. Have them put the puzzle together and read the story back to you.

As you watch television, listen to music, and play games, talk about likes, differences, and strategies; share what you are thinking. Discuss decisions and why you made them.

Reading

As soon as your children learn to read, have them read books to you. If they seem to have difficulty, read aloud simultaneously with them for at least 15 minutes every day. This gives them confidence in their reading. Sitting on their left side also encourages eye movement, left to right (the way books are written).

Continue reading books to your children, even after they learn to read. Children can comprehend at a higher level than they can read for themselves.

As your children develop their reading abilities, provide them with books they can easily read. Their teachers and your city and school librarian will have many book suggestions. Magazines, joke books, comic books . . . all are okay. They're reading! Encourage them to read both aloud and silently. When you hear them laugh or see them cry as they read, ask them to tell you what the book said. Emotions enhance learning (in fact, recent brain research suggests no learning occurs unless emotions are involved), so encourage your children to develop "relationships" with what they read. When book heroes or heroines become their imaginary friends, encourage them.

When they complete a book, have them tell you the story. If they have trouble remembering, ask them to tell you what happened every few pages or at the end of each chapter.

If they begin a book but find it boring, let them get a new book (but don't let them make this a habit). You want them to love reading.

Developing Skills

As your children move into trying to understand nonfiction material, they need to develop new skills of comprehension. They need to be able to read a paragraph and understand what it means, in the same way the author intended it. They need to be able to think as they read so they can test everything they read against their value system and what they know to be true. By the time they enter college, they will need to be able to do this with at least 100 pages per day per class.

Reading to Learn

When Jeff started getting into the music of his generation, I had a great opportunity to help him think about lyrics and practice making healthy decisions. Because I believe music is important and children need their own music, we shared. On Monday, Wednesday, and Friday, Jeff got to select the radio station we listened to in the car. On Tuesday, Thursday, and Saturday, I got to. On Sunday, we could negotiate.

Both of us had veto power. If he hated something I was listening to, or if I hated something he was listening to, we would turn off the radio or change the station.

When I found his music offensive, I would explain to him what in the lyrics offended me. I believe that we become what we put into our minds, that we begin to think of that which we feed our brains as normal. Growing up, I crooned Elvis's "Treat me like a fool, treat me mean and cruel, but love me." I am an Elvis fan, but those lyrics fed my mind things I don't want to ever believe are normal. A recent study by the Rand Corporation confirmed that teenagers who regularly listen to music lyrics with explicit references to sex are more likely to be involved in premature sexual activity.

As Jeff matured, he would be listening to his music, and suddenly the station would change. I would say, "Why did you change the station?" He would laugh and say, "Trust me, Mom. You wouldn't like the words to that song."

I'm not naïve enough to think he didn't listen when I wasn't with him. After all, he could turn off the song before it even got to the words because he knew what was coming. But I do know that I taught him to think about what he puts into his mind.

Try the following comprehension strategies to help your children become critical, thinking readers. For these comprehension exercises, be more concerned with your children understanding what they are reading than you are with their reading speed. If they struggle, choral-read each paragraph rather than asking them to read to you.

- Help them when they struggle; this is not a test, it is an effort to make them confident and competent readers.
- Have your child go through a paragraph and "X" out every word that isn't important to the meaning of the sentence.
- Have your child look over the pictures, captions, and headings of a text before beginning to read.
- Have your child read a paragraph and tell you what she read in different words.
- Have your child develop three questions for each paragraph she reads.
- Have your child predict what will happen in the next paragraph of a story. Then read to see if the prediction was accurate.
- When he reads a word he doesn't understand, help him read it within the context of the sentence and see if he can guess the meaning. Then check the dictionary to see if his assumption was right. Beginning readers need to clarify words and concepts they don't understand.
- Read a story to your child and have him draw a picture of what you read.
- Read a story to your child and have him act out what you just read.
- Read a story to your child and have him paraphrase the entire story into one sentence.
- Read a story and have your child change the ending. See how many endings she can create to the same story.
- Read a story, substituting your child's name for one of the characters. Then reverse; have your child tell the story putting your name in.

- Discuss a story where a character solved a problem. See how many different ways your child can discover for solving the same problem.

- Read a paragraph to her out loud. Look up and tell her, in your own words, what the paragraph said. Have her read the next paragraph out loud to you. Then have her tell you, in her own words, what the paragraph said. If she needs help, she may look back at the paragraph and try to find key points.

- After your child is comfortable with the above technique, add two new dimensions to it. After paraphrasing the paragraph, have him create three questions from the paragraph that you have to answer. Then, before you take your turn to read, have him predict what will be said in the next paragraph.

- When you get into more difficult content, read a paragraph with your child and have him write in one sentence what the entire paragraph had to say. This is a great test preparation technique.

- Have your child read a story silently while you read the same story silently. Then discuss what you believe that meant, and have your child share what he believes it meant. Now trade; have your child share first.

- Invite friends over to study. Have the friends each read the same section and discuss what they learned from it. Share key ideas.

- Try to find three to five key concepts in the passage.

- Identify the three to five central themes or concepts in a passage and then turn them into a song, a rap, a visual, or a dance.

- After reading a book, watch the movie. Discuss how they were alike and how they were different. Talk about which story line you prefer and why the screenwriters might have changed the story. Explain that screenwriters need to "condense" material because a book is too long for a two-hour movie. They use the same skills to do this that you use to condense a paragraph into one sentence.

Advanced Comprehension Techniques

When your children begin studying history and science, I recommend an age-old technique conceived by F. P. Robinson in *Effective Study:* The SQ3R. Simply, this means S-Survey; Q-Question; R-Read; R-Recite; R-Review:

Survey. Before beginning a chapter, survey its contents. Read the introduction, main headings, footnotes, pictures, charts, captions, and summary questions.

Question. Go back to the beginning and turn every major heading into a question.

Read. Read the section.

Recite. Go back to your question and recite the answer. If you can't answer your question, either create a more appropriate question or reread the section.

Review. When you have completed the chapter, review by answering all the questions. Study only what you have forgotten.

The RESIT Technique

When your children are having trouble comprehending, they may be so frustrated that they quit trying. When that happens, read it alongside them and have them estimate the percent they think they understood (they'll understand the concept of percentages around fourth grade; before then, skip the first step):

"Did you understand 100 percent? 2 percent? 20 percent?"

"Of what you understood (say 20 percent), what did it say?"

"Of what you didn't understand, what are two specific things you don't know?"

Talk about the above questions, adding your paraphrase and what you thought was confusing about the passage. Then have them reread it. Then together create questions to ask in class the next day about the passage.

This is one of my favorite strategies because it makes it okay for students not to understand 100 percent. When they don't understand something, they have a tendency to quit reading. Usually, what has really happened is they don't know the meaning of one or two words so they throw the entire passage away.

A teacher friend of mine has her students write on the paper, "I don't know how to do this one." She tells me children can't think in "blank spaces"; this empowers them to skip what they don't know and go on. Often, after they have answered the other questions, they can come back to the problem that caused them grief and easily finish their work.

Effective Comprehension Strategies

I recently taught alternative approaches to learning to a ninth-grade class. At the conclusion, students wrote what they had learned. One commented, "Now I know if I don't understand something, I can draw it!"

Yes! And you can sing it or act it out, too!

When children struggle for comprehension, all effective comprehension strategies have the following common elements:

1. They place the burden of work on the child, not the parent or the teacher. The child searches for meaning.
2. They go over material two or three times in two or three different ways. For example, you read it, you identify key words, you draw it. You do more than one thing with the content.
3. They are always interactive. In the written strategies, the child journals to be interactive with himself; in the visual approaches, the child draws a picture that he may share, involving peer interaction or that he may use himself, involving interaction through intrapersonal intelligence; and in the discussion exercises, the child interacts with a

parent or with a peer. Communication is always a part of comprehension.

Reading Speed

Young children should read books that are easy to read so they can develop their speech and feel successful. Read with them, read to them, have them read to you. Cheer them for their accomplishments. Most will reach automaticity and read at recommended speeds using these strategies.

The California School Leadership Academy states that elementary-school children should read approximately sixty-five words a minute. Middle-school children should read approximately 120 words a minute. High-school students should read at about 200 words a minute. Before they leave for college (but not before eleventh grade), I recommend that your children take a speed-reading course. Speed-readers reach between 800 and 2,000 words a minute. Reading will be central to everything they do in life. College students need to read 80 to 120 pages per day for each class.

Your children who read below the standard speeds probably are not at automaticity in their reading yet. This means that helping them build speed is vital to their success.

When they are reading well, in approximately third grade, have them read for one minute and count the words read. If they are not at the speed they should be, have a contest with them. Say, "I'm going to time you for one minute. This time, when you read, see how fast you can read it."

If they're extremely slow readers, read the passage aloud with them. Build speed together while they gain confidence.

If they are beyond third grade, you can use "speed sprints" to help them read better every once in a while. Say, "Now read for only thirty seconds, and let's see if in thirty seconds you can read as far as you read in one minute." They read for thirty seconds and multiply the words read by two. Cheer for them each time they read a few words faster.

Have them reread the same page several times, trying to read faster each time.

As long as they are improving, continue to reread the same material but shorten the time read:

One minute on new material to get base speed
Thirty seconds on the same material times two
Twenty seconds on the same material times three
Fifteen seconds on the same material times four
Twelve seconds on the same material times five
Repeat twelve seconds
Repeat twelve seconds
One minute on new material to get new sustained speed

As long as they are improving, follow this formula every night for one week; repeat it one month later. Continue to work on reading speed once a month until they are within the above norms.

If they suddenly decrease in reading speed, they have probably fatigued their eyes. **Do not press on**; try it again another day when they're fresh. If this happens often, have them checked by a vision professional (see Chapter 23).

Dealing with Problems

If something seems to detract from learning, remove it until you find the cause. For example, hand-writing was tedious for my son. To alleviate this, I drilled him orally and he used the computer for most writing assignments.

If there is a difference between their silent reading skills and their verbal skills, or if they reverse letters in words or skip small words, they may need glasses or vision therapy.

If there is a difference in performance between morning and evening, it may signify a vision problem, or you may simply have an introverted personality who is in need of rest.

If there is a difference in performance before or after eating, there may be a food allergy or blood sugar problem.

If they do better on written work than oral, they may have a slight hearing disorder.

See Chapter 23 for where to find help.

 Every child can learn to read. If we do our job well, every child will also learn to love reading!

Certainly reading comprehension is more complex than it sounds here. But that leads us to the experts. If you have used these techniques and worked with the school but your child is still not reading at grade level, enroll her in a reading tutorial program (see Chapter 23). Reading is vital to success in life. Every child can learn to read. If we do our job well, every child will also learn to love reading!

REFLECTION

Jeff was struggling to find the answer for his seventh grade science class homework. After letting him struggle for a while, I sat down with him and asked, "Have you read the headings to look up where to find the answer?" He had.

I said, "Have you looked at the pictures to find a clue for the answer and read the captions underneath the pictures?" He had.

"Have you skimmed the text for key words?" Yes, he had done that, too.

When I was satisfied that he had done what he could do, I sat down to look for the answer to the question. I ended up scanning the entire text, and I couldn't find the answer either. A friend who was a seventh-grade science teacher at another school dropped by as we were in the midst of our quest. I turned to him and said, "We're struggling to find an answer. What's the answer to—" and repeated the question. His response was, "Oh, that's easy." He told us the answer. I said, "Find it for me in the book." He skimmed through the book, then chuckled a little and said, "It's not in this edition. The homework question was written with last year's book."

I wrote Jeff's science teacher a note—yes, it was a nice one. I'm a teacher, too, so I understand the workload.

If your child can't find an answer and you can't find an answer, it's probably time for a little communication with the school.

16

How to Study for Tests

"I want to help my children prepare for tests, but I don't know where to begin. It seems that every class and every teacher is different. Is there an easy way to figure out what to study?"

Ah, what a wonderful question! Where do I begin?

My first experience with student test anxiety was in my typing class (in the olden days before we taught keyboarding on computers). A young, inexperienced teacher, I walked into the class about week three and announced excitedly, "Today we will take our first timed writing test."

Forty students simultaneously inhaled and stiffened, and I thought, "What do I do with that?"

I learned to help them breathe deeply, wiggle their shoulders, and shake their hands to relieve the tension. I also learned that if I told a joke just before they began, they were less anxious. Laughter is a great tension-reliever.

 Examinations are formidable, even to the best prepared, for the greatest fool may ask more than the wisest man can answer.

—Charles Caleb Colton (1780-1832)

There is a plethora of materials on objective test-taking techniques and techniques for preparing for the pre-college entrance examinations. In this chapter, the focus is on how

163

parents can help their children prepare for tests. As your children mature, work from the manuals that devote several volumes to the nuances of test-taking techniques.

Taking tests will provide your children with many challenges. Some students use improper study techniques for the type of exam they will be taking. Some students study correctly but suffer from test anxiety that results in poor performance. Still other students misinterpret test questions and overlook key words.

Ask the Questions

Make your review match the test. Will your child be tested with an objective test, an essay test, or a combination of the two?

Help your child formulate questions about a test to ask prior to studying for the examination:

What kinds of questions will be on the test? You study differently for objective tests than you do for an essay exam. Your child needs to know before he begins whether to study details or concepts.

What chapters/concepts will the test cover? One testing principle is "divide and conquer." Study only what you will be tested on; study only what you don't know. If your child's teacher provides a study sheet, make sure your child knows that information well.

How many questions are on the test? Knowing exactly what to expect will serve to relieve surface test anxiety. For example, if your child knows that the test will be 100 questions, he won't have to look at the long exam and worry, "Can I get through this in the time allotted?" He has already had those thoughts and knows to dig in.

Do all questions count the same number of points? Sometimes teachers count one point each for true/false, five points each for short answer, and twenty-five or fifty points for the one essay question at the end. That means the one essay question may be worth 50 percent of the grade. If that is the case, have your child answer the essay question first, then the short answer. Finish with the true/false. Yes, that may reverse the teacher's order, but it ensures that your child doesn't lose points by not getting to the essay question. If he has no time left for the essay question, he could receive a failing grade even if he answered all objective test questions correctly.

Encourage your child to ask questions during the exam about anything he doesn't understand.

If your child doesn't know how to answer a question, have him skip that question and find one he can answer. If he has time, he can go back when he finishes the rest of the test. Often, he will gain clues to the answer of that question from the other test questions. Too often, when one question stumps a child, he'll quit and miss the following questions, too.

Objective Tests

Objective tests are most frequently composed of multiple choice, true/false, and matching test items. These tests are called objective because the same examination paper corrected by several different people will yield the same score in each case. An essay graded by several different people, however, will usually yield several different scores, some widely divergent.

Objective examinations are designed to test your children's ability to reason logically from evidence, organize material, recognize similarities and differences, make fine distinctions, or apply general concepts to particular problems.

Multiple Choice Questions

Multiple choice exam questions typically begin with a statement and then ask that you complete that statement by choosing the best answer or the answer that doesn't belong.

Predict. To master multiple choice exams, try to guess the answer before you read the choices. For example, how would you finish these sentences?

As a child, Walt Disney was:
When it freezes, water:
The primary reason for the Civil War was:
The primary source of power for homes is:

Predicting the end of the sentence before you read the choices will likely lead you to the best choice when you read the options.

Read the question. Sometimes our children try to answer the question without reading the introduction. The introduction to multiple choice questions usually sets conditions for the test. For example, in the statement above, "The primary source for power in homes is," the answer for today would likely be *electricity*. If the introduction stated, "Assume you live in the early 1800s," the answer might instead be *wood*, perhaps even *coal*.

Eliminate. If you don't know the answer, look over the choices. Eliminate the most obviously wrong answer. Continue eliminating as long as you can. Select from the answers you have left.

Sometimes the answer to the question is actually contained in the paragraph that leads into the questions.

True/False Questions

Remind your children to ask how their teacher will grade true/false questions. On most tests students will take in school, they can guess if they don't know the answer to true/false questions because there is no extra penalty if they get it wrong. Occasionally, however, a teacher will subtract items answered incorrectly from those answered correctly. For example, normally if there are 100 questions and you miss ten, you get 90 percent. If, however, they subtract the number right from the number wrong, you only get 80 percent: you got ninety right and ten wrong; ninety minus ten is eighty.

Most school exams are graded without a penalty for guessing. The pre-college entrance examinations, however, will penalize you. Make sure your students know how to study for exams rather than guessing before they take their pre-college tests.

The whole truth. Mark a statement true only if it is 100 percent true. If half of the question is true and half is false, the entire question is false. If one word makes it not true 100 percent of the time, the entire question is false:

"High unemployment is *the* cause of crime in the ghetto area" is false.

"High unemployment is *one* cause of crime in the ghetto area" is true.

Never say never. Words such as *always, never, every,* and *none* leave no room for exceptions. Read these questions carefully; most of the time they are false.

Beware more than one. Composite-statement questions are those true/false statements that contain more than one thought. When one portion of the statement is true and one portion of the statement is false, the entire question is false:

"The Golden Gate Bridge is in San Francisco, the capital of California" is false.

Beware the negative. Often test-writers will sandwich the word "not" between two normal associations. That one word makes the statement false. If your children hurry through the exam and overlook the little words, they may miss the question.

Know the teacher. Sometimes our children will read too much into a test question. It is important to ascertain what the teacher intended rather than to overanalyze the questions.

Matching Questions

Matching questions have a list of items on one side of the paper that are to be matched to their counterparts (author, definition, etc.) in another column. Have your children start with what they know. Then they have fewer items to choose from for those that they question.

Essay Test Techniques

You may find that your children do well on objective tests but freeze on an essay test. Or you may find that your children do well on essay tests but poorly on an objective test. Their preference may depend on their personality. Objective tests ask about details; essay tests are more thematic.

Schools currently use a rubric to grade essay exams. The rubric delineates the grade-appropriate writing skills and nuances of the writing prompt. Although rubrics vary widely, they will look something like this:

Ask your teacher for the rubric so you can see how your child will be graded.

My favorite essay-test preparation technique is clustering. Clustering is quite similar to using a graphic organizer except that students are generating the content, rather than taking notes on content presented by someone else. In the cluster technique, the students spend the first few minutes on an essay question organizing their thoughts via a cluster. They then use their cluster notes to develop their paragraphs in an organized fashion.

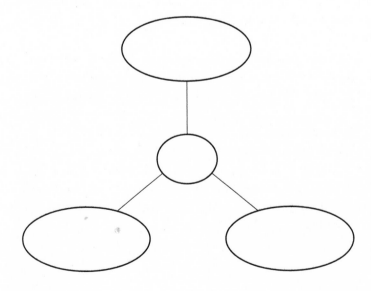

	1	2	3	4	5
Grammar	Essay written with grammatical correctness; no major errors of punctuation.	Essay written with no more than 1 or 2 grammatical errors.	Essay written with simple grammatical structure. Few errors.	Essay contains grammatical or spelling errors.	Essay contains fragments and run-on sentences. Spelling errors. Poor use of grammar.
Content	Essay shows deep grasp of meaning. Good flow. Cause and effect analysis thorough. Shows thematic insights.	Essay shows grasp of meaning. Cause and effect analysis thorough. General thematic understanding.	Essay shows overall understanding of concepts. Missing cause and effect. Average thematic support.	Essay shows shallow understanding of content. Poor thematic support.	Essay vague and general. Does not show grasp of thematic concepts.

In a cluster, the topic is in the center of the page. As thoughts come, they are organized around the topic. Let's say, for simplicity, that your essay question is "How did the Indians survive when they lived on the plains?" As in a concept map, your topic goes in the middle of the page.

As your thoughts come, you write them down around your topic. As they begin to naturally fall into categories, you cluster them.

Let's say your first thought was they lived in teepees or cliff dwellings. That goes in one circle.

Next, you think, they hunted for food. Another circle.

Next, you think, "They wore animal skins to keep warm." Another circle.

Next, you think, "They had to use bows and arrows because they didn't have guns yet." "Bows and arrows" goes in the cluster with "hunted for food." It is related to the topic.

Then you think, "They slept on the ground, covered with pelts from the animals." Add that to the circle about teepees or cliff dwellings.

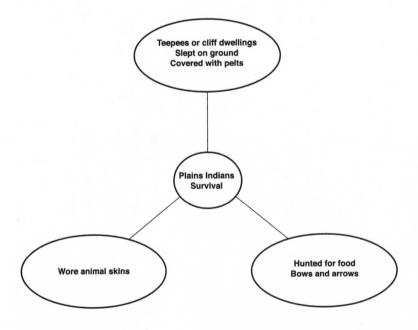

You now have the beginnings of three clusters: How they got their food; how they kept warm; how they slept. These can form your three paragraphs.

The advantage of using clustering is that it allows our children to "splash down" their thoughts in the first few minutes (no more than five) when their thoughts are coming rapidly and randomly. As they splash down their thoughts they can organize them into categories that later become paragraphs; thus their thoughts are organized before they begin to write. Their writing has better flow that way.

Reducing Test Anxiety

Of course, a little bit of test anxiety is good; it provides the motivation that causes our children to study. Too much test anxiety, however, can cause them to freeze.

One of the first keys to reducing test anxiety is adequate preparation. As we deal with test anxiety, we should teach our children, among other things, how to study, how to feel confident about their preparation for a test, how to quiz one another, and how to utilize relaxation strategies we know to be effective.

Our children don't eagerly approach us with the news "I froze on the test." They simply flunk another test and feel as though they are personal failures because of it. We need to be on the lookout for things that don't make sense to us: they knew the material and appeared to understand concepts when we reviewed the night before the exam, yet failed the test over the same material; they do very well with their homework, but do poorly on the test over the same material. Ask, "Does this grade make sense?" If the test grade is lower than our perception of our child's understanding, there may be a test-anxiety problem.

Of course, these may also be signs of other, related problems. For example, the student may have a visual perceptual difficulty rather than, or in addition to, test anxiety. These are difficult problems to discover and often require screening by a specialist in learning/reading disabilities. Students may have the knowledge, but poor reading skills. Students whose native language is not English often have discrepancies between verbal and written performance while they transition. It may be that there is a mismatch between the test and teaching style. To help your children who suffer from test anxiety, try the following:

- Have them use good study strategies following the Learning Principles from Chapter 21. That gives them confidence.
- Have them close their eyes and take three slow, deep breaths before they begin the test.
- Have them envision themselves answering every question the right way.
- Have them study using mnemonic devices. They serve as a right-brain trigger into the left-brain memory bank.
- Have them flex their muscles; then relax them two or three times.
- Have them study with friends.

Pre-College Testing

Those who are in the Scholastic Aptitude Test (SAT) or the American College Test (ACT) business tell us you really can't prepare a student for these exams; they are the outgrowth of prior learning. My experience has been that test preparation increases scores an average of 200 points. I strongly recommend that you prepare your child for the SAT and/or the ACT.

The primary difference between the SAT and the ACT is in the focus. The SAT test is considered a general intelligence type test, whereas the ACT is considered to be based on school curriculum. Just because they are different approaches to testing, some students will perform better on one test than on the other. I usually encourage students, if a test grade is important based on the university they plan to attend, to sign up for and take both exams and use their highest score.

I also strongly recommend that students take the PSAT and/ or PACT (P = Preliminary; it is considered a "practice" for the real thing) in either tenth or eleventh grade. This gives them time to receive their scores and know whether or not they need to take a test-preparatory course in math, language arts, or both. I've found it also is an effective counseling tool to relieve student test anxiety.

The first question to ask yourself is whether or not you need to worry about this test. That depends on the college your child has chosen and her high school grades in academic subjects. The higher her grade point average, the lower her test score can be. For some colleges, the tests are a formality, and the score is not tied to admissions. For others, improving a test score could mean the difference in whether or not your child is admitted to the college or university of her choice. Her high school counselor can advise you. Your child's college of choice will have its test score requirements on its Web site.

There are a number of outstanding commercial programs for SAT and ACT preparation. As a first step, I recommend you purchase a practice test book, found in the reference section in your local bookstore. Currently, my favorite is *11 Practice Tests for the New SAT and PSAT* by Princeton Review. Have your child take one test and score it. Go over the scoring sheet and discover how many points she lost by guessing (remember, these tests penalize a wrong answer). Then review each missed test question and discuss strategies for arriving at a right answer. After that, have her take the next practice test using the new strategies. Continue this process until she is comfortable with the test format and questions, and until she achieves her desired test score.

Those students who need a high score on the SAT and/or ACT and who don't test well will probably want to take a formal test-preparation class. Many agencies offer these courses; they are effective. Most community colleges and university extensions also offer such preparation. However, I am personally concerned about the amount of test anxiety that is generated over the SAT/ACT requirement. According to researchers Uri Treisman and Harold Hodgkinson, these test scores do not correlate to college or university graduation rates. Given this, they are a formality of admission. Have your child decide which university he wants to attend and check the corresponding grade point and SAT/ACT score needed to be eligible for admission and/or priority admission. Then prepare him to the extent that is necessary for him to gain that admission. Although he can retake the test as many times as he wants to in order to earn a higher grade, if he did well and is admissible to his college of choice, there is no reason for him to retake it for a higher score.

General Test Preparation Strategies

If your students follow the guidelines in the preceding chapters on taking notes, their test preparation is simple. They simply review their notes and relate them to their textbooks.

If they used the wide left margin with a test question, key word, or memory key, they cover up the right-hand side that contains notes and see if they can remember the content based on their prompt in the left-hand column. If they can, they don't need to study. If they can't, they uncover the notes to find the answers and drill themselves in sets of three using many modalities. If the test will be objective, they make sure they know the important names, dates, places, and relationships. If it will be essay, they rehearse the themes, relationships, and application principles.

If they took notes using a concept map, they review their symbols to see if they can remember the details. If so, they don't need to study. If not, they drill themselves in sets of three using multiple modalities.

If the test is over math problems, they work through one each of the type of problem that will appear on the test. If they know how to do the problems, they don't need to study. If they don't know how, they work practice problems that represent those that will be on the test. They continue working problems, learning from their errors, until they get three right.

If the teacher provides a review or study guide, they highlight categories in one color, key points in another. They can have someone quiz them on the key points. If they know them, they don't need to study. If they don't know them, they drill in sets of three.

If they are confusing two or three key concepts, they (probably with your help or the help of friends) should create a mnemonic device to help them remember. They can sing a song, draw a picture, create an absurd visual image, make an acronym out of the first letters of each item, rap, dance . . . the list is as vast as their imaginations. When they take the test, they remember their mnemonic device, which triggers their memories of what they wish to remember.

REFLECTION

My first year of teaching, I got pneumonia and was out of school for two weeks shortly after the second semester started. When I returned, I had lost the class; my substitute had let them just sit and talk.

It was time to review for the mid-term, and they ignored my review. When I graded their exams, 14 students obviously had cheated on an essay exam. It was almost as bad as one student writing, "I don't understand," And the student sitting next to her writing, "I don't understand, either."

When something that widespread happens, you have to take drastic measures; but always, there must be a way to atone. I lowered every grade, gave unsatisfactory citizenship marks, and promised them these grades would be deleted at the semester end if it never happened again.

I got only two phone calls from parents. Both asked why the low grades. Both listened while I explained: "You have a wonderful daughter, but we've had an unfortunate situation." Both, then, said, "You told me the same thing my daughter did. I really called to say thank you for caring enough to stop a problem before it became a habit."

No one received a lower semester grade.

17

How to Develop Lifelong Learners

"My daughter gets good grades, but I want more for her than grades. I want her to think. I want her to make wise life choices."

You express the heart of a parent. Here are some tools.

I watched in the years leading up to Jeff's high-school graduation as the children of dear friends struggled in college with alcohol or drug abuse. They were raised with the same value system I embraced. I sought help to prevent Jeff from making these poor decisions.

During Jeff's senior year of high school, I gave him full responsibility for his life decisions. Of course, he needed to tell me where he would be, and to call if he was going to be late, and he still had to negotiate for the family car. I maintained full veto power if his grades suffered, if he began to do harmful things, or he failed to do his homework.

When I thought he was making a poor decision, I discussed it with him—sometimes passionately. But unless the decision was dangerous, he was allowed to make it, whether or not I agreed with him. When it worked out well, I admitted I had been wrong. When it worked out poorly, we talked about what he could learn in order to make a better decision next time.

Of course, I watched his behavior closely. Teenagers are under constant pressure to slack off at school, and to try sex, drugs, and alcohol. Had any of these become issues, his new freedom would immediately have been pulled. I am thankful

I never had to deal with them. Jeff gained the "freshman ten pounds" at home on sodas rather than at college on beer.

Ultimately, college was fun for him, not traumatic, because he was able to make decisions after having had experience in resisting peer pressure.

I recently discussed the issue of homework with a friend who expressed his concern. In his children's school, every parent is assertive about education. He said that parents would actually cheat for their children in order to earn better grades so the children could gain admission to more prestigious schools.

The sad part about this behavior is that such tactics backfire:

- Children don't learn how to compete if their parents compete for them.
- Children don't learn how to study if their parents study for them.
- Children don't learn from their mistakes if their parents don't allow them to make mistakes.
- Children don't learn how to manage guilt and other emotions if their parents carry their guilt for them (or don't appropriately teach them the difference between right and wrong).

To develop lifelong learners, you need to be a role model; you need to allow your children to experience both success and failure.

Lifelong Learners Are Made by Example

If you want your children to be curious, you must continue to wonder at the world, to explore, to try new things, and to learn. If you want your children to read, read to them; read for pleasure yourself; ask them to read to you. If you want your children to be problem-solvers, share your problems with them and ask their advice. One standard checklist item to help determine whether you were raised in a dysfunctional family states: Thinks "normal" is "perfect."

Lifelong Learners Are Made by Encouraging Creativity and Effort

If you want your children to be lifelong learners, cheer their imaginations. Hang their pictures in a prominent place. Go to their games and performances. Be their greatest cheerleader.

Lifelong Learners Are Motivated from Within

If you want your children to be self-motivated, allow them to make mistakes and to learn from the consequences. Let them try new, perhaps crazy, things. The self-motivated students are risk-takers. Risk-takers sometimes get hurt. Pick up their pieces, don't scold them for trying something new. The song entitled "The Rose" has a line that says, "It's the soul afraid of dying that never learns to live."

Lifelong Learners Are Decision-Makers

If you want your children to make wise lifelong decisions, you must allow them to practice by making little decisions. As they mature, allow them to make more of their own decisions. Remember that they become legal adults at age 18. If they are given increasing responsibility and the right to make decisions as they mature, that adult responsibility will be natural—the next step. If they have not had that freedom, they often make poor personal decisions their first years away from home. Sometimes the consequences of these decisions last a lifetime.

Lifelong Learners Achieve Success

Psychologist Dr. James Dobson suggests that you discover your child's natural interest and/or talent early in life and help him develop it. This talent may be in playing tennis, singing, doing woodwork, painting or drawing, excelling academically, or any number of things. When you develop them to the level of competency in one area, they can compete with the best. They have a successful experience to fall back on when times are tough. Dr. Dobson's father taught him to play tennis; it is a great stress-reliever for him today. See to it that your child can do something exceptionally well.

Lifelong Learners Pursue Their Dream

When they believe in and enjoy what they are doing, they put themselves into it. When they are working for a parent's dream, they lack inner motivation. They may achieve success, but they will not achieve happiness.

Lifelong Learners Assume Responsibility

We parents are great co-dependents. The best test I know for co-dependency is to ask yourself two questions:

- Can my child do this for himself?
- Should my child do this for himself?

If the answer to both of those questions is yes, you need to say, "The ball's in your court." If this means earning a low grade, they need to learn from it. If this means failing to turn in the assignment, they need to pay the consequences. If, however, the answer to one of those questions is no, it is our responsibility as parents to jump in and help them out. We do that not by doing it for them, but by empowering them to do it for themselves.

 The best way to give advice to your child is to find out what they want to do and then advise them to do it.

—Winston Churchill

···················· REFLECTION ····················

Jeff started college when cell phones were a luxury instead of a toy, but he had learned my telephone credit card number well. He called often (which I loved), and always with a comment of, "I called Uncle Bob. I called my friend Melanie. I called Grandma."

I would say to him, "Jeff, you're going to get a phone bill. You need to be careful making all those long-distance calls."

He got his first dorm phone bill, and it was only $30. I thought, "I need to check into this college's phone plan, because they sure have a better deal than I do."

Then I got my phone bill. Suddenly it all made sense; he had used my credit card for his many phone calls. I sent him his portion of the bill. I told him he could call me collect, or call me on the credit card ten times a day, and I would be happy to pay the bill. But when he called other people, he had to pay for it.

Calls continued for one more month, and I got a phone call. "Mom, my phone bill is $120!" We chatted, and I laughed with him about it. I let him continue to talk. Pretty soon I heard noise in the background. He said, "My friends want to know if you're bawling me out."

I said, "Tell them no, but I'm not bailing you out either."

The phone was in his roommate's name. It took Jeff three months to pay his roommate off. He learned a great lesson.

I told him he was on the right road to adulthood. First he gets custody of a telephone bill. Then he gets custody of a car payment. If he manages that well, someday he might actually gain custody of a mortgage!

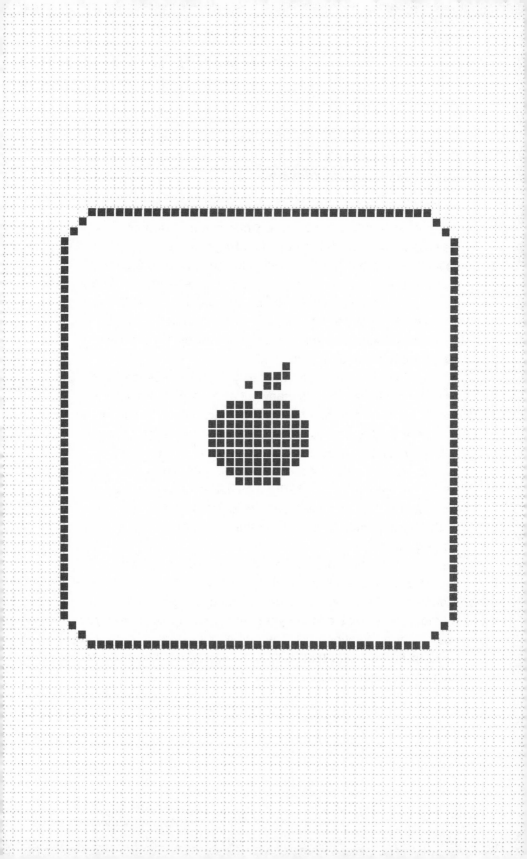

SECTION III

RESPONDING TO COMMON STUDENT COMPLAINTS

Many jokes are told about the "preacher's kid" who causes so much trouble the preacher's sermons are compromised. My son is the epitome of the "teacher's kid." He was such a difficult student that there were times when it embarrassed me to tell his teachers what I do for a living.

Jeff had a great kindergarten teacher. As we talked, she kept referring to him as bright. I was recovering from some personal trauma and still in "survival mode." I commented, "It's funny. You keep calling him bright, but I've never cared about that. I just want him to be happy."

She replied, "I don't know what he knew before he started kindergarten."

"He knew the alphabet, but none of the sounds. I tried to teach him, but he didn't seem to want to learn them, so I quit."

"Then he's not bright; he's brilliant. He's ignored everything I've said, and he knows them all now."

 School is important, but your personal relationship with your child is far more important than completing a homework assignment.

We cannot control the time our children spend in school. We are bound to their reports of the day's learnings and homework assignments, plus our occasional contact with their teachers. How do we sort out the truth? How much pressure do we use? Which side do we take in a disagreement? When do we intervene?

I wish there were clear-cut answers, but our children are far too complex for that! Rather, this section will offer guidelines for you to personalize.

School is important, but your personal relationship with your child is far more important than completing a homework assignment.

Your Child Wants to Learn

As you review these chapters, keep in mind the following principle from the Caine Learning Institute: "The search for meaning is innate." This means that we know beyond a doubt that there is no such thing as a child who doesn't care; there is no such thing as a child who wants to fail; there is no such thing as a child who would rather throw his life away than succeed. When our children struggle, they need our help and encouragement.

Never give up.

·················· **REFLECTION** ··················

Jeff started school in a K-1 combination class. At the end of our third parent conference, Mrs. Patterson said, "Maybe this is my problem. Come back tomorrow."

The next day I visited his classroom. Mrs. Patterson said, "Jeff, show your mother what you learned today."

Jeff proceeded to read me the entire first-grade pre-primer.

Jeff already knew what the kindergartners were learning, so he had tuned them out. Instead, he was eavesdropping on the first-grade reading lessons; they were learning what he was ready to learn next. Since he was in a K-1 combination, Mrs. Patterson simply switched reading groups.

What we observed as "strange behavior" was actually a child "searching for meaning." He already knew his sounds so he wandered around the room trying to learn something new.

18

It's Boring, Boring, Boring!

"My daughter's sense of logic amazes me. She says, 'Why should I do my homework? I already know that stuff; we learned it last year. Besides, it's so boring!

'Actually, the class is boring, too. It's so boring that I don't even care if I get a good grade.'

Help!"

First of all, let's admit it. Some classes *are* boring—to some students, and/or because of some teachers. Don't argue with them; 100 percent true or not, they believe it. With that in mind, we need to provide our students with strategies for making a boring class more interesting (not try to talk them into liking it).

We also need to tell them that everything in life has something that is boring or tedious. For example, I don't enjoy doing the dishes or taking out the trash. I don't usually learn great things while I do them. For that matter, I don't enjoy making my bed—but I hate to crawl into a bed that is disheveled. And if I don't do it, it won't get done.

While we're at it, I love the creative process of writing. The rewrites and editing aren't so fun. But I love the "new and improved" finished product. There is a slogan among writers: "An editor is the person who keeps a writer from making a fool of himself (or herself) in front of the world." I submit to the editing because I really fear the alternative!

All of life is a blend of the exciting and the boring . . . and sometimes the painful. Your children cannot change their teachers so they must change themselves. There are strategies for getting through a boring class—strategies that will produce a win-win. Win-win is really the only way to do life.

Use Active Learning Strategies

To help make a boring class more interesting, suggest your child try one or all of the following, depending on personality.

Take Notes

This will keep their hands busy, help them focus, and facilitate learning. It will give them something to think about rather than how boring the class is. There is actually a spinoff benefit for them when they take notes. We write approximately twenty words a minute, talk upwards of 200 words a minute, and think thousands of words a minute. Taking class notes uses our thousands of thoughts to listen to the 200 words and figure out how to get them down to their essence, the twenty that are most important. Having your children take notes in class will not only alleviate the boredom complaint, it will increase learning.

Ask Questions

Help them create clever (but not obnoxious) questions to ask. This will allow them to use their imaginations to create interest in the class.

Teach It on Paper

Have them design a plan to teach the class in an interesting way. When they sit in a boring class, they tend to disrupt class, cause trouble, write notes to friends, or tune out. Have them, instead, try to relate what the teacher is saying to how they would teach it, if they were the teacher. They can make this part of their notes, using a three-column approach. Label one column "Memory Key," one "Lecture," and one "Reaction," then do separate entries under the appropriate column for "The Teacher said . . . " and "I would . . . "

Three-Column Notes

Memory Key	Lecture	Reaction
Why was Tevye opposed to Tzeitel's marriage to Motel?	Tevye believed in matchmakers. Tevye wanted his daughters to marry money.	If I were the teacher . . . I'd sing out all my questions . . . And I'd ask the kids to answer them in pun. Deedle dydle dodle deedle dum

Do It to Music
Compose a song about the content. If it's *really* boring, have them make it a *slow* song.

Draw a Picture
Draw a picture (or create a cartoon) of the class content. If they use this technique, they may have to explain it to the teacher to prove they were listening rather than doodling.

Take Creative Notes
Make your class notes in the form of a storyboard, or write your own play from what the teacher says.

Use Color
Find a way to color-code the lecture. This will keep the creative juices flowing and help with focus.

Make It Your Favorite
Teach your children to act as though each class is their favorite (and to see how creative they can be in convincing their teacher). "But," you say, "it wouldn't be the truth; wouldn't I be

teaching them to lie?" Probably not. You see, positive energy generates enthusiasm, which generates positive energy. Most students really learn to love a class when they devote that much attention to it.

Find the Real Issue

Now, back to charges of boredom. As you work with your children, check out what is behind the charges. Sometimes it's true. Sometimes it points to other issues, especially if they are bored with other subjects or with things they normally enjoy. Look for:

Feelings of Incompetence

When our children don't understand something, when they repeatedly try and fail, they finally reach a point where they subconsciously think, "I'd rather be belligerent than stupid." With that, their behavior becomes passive or aggressive. Check out Chapter 20 for strategies to intervene.

Buried Grief

When life has been traumatic for us, we enter "survival mode." We reach a point where we are exhausted. We enter a mild state of depression that may manifest itself as "I don't care." In children, there is a "sleeper effect" of grief; if not dealt with, grief is buried. Buried grief is buried alive. It will periodically consume them and interfere with learning. Average grieving time is two years. If they have buried grief, it can remain buried for many years. Those who bury grief don't function at 100 percent. Living a life with buried grief is like carrying a heavy load; it slows you down in everything you do. If you have had trauma over the last several years, consider grief recovery classes for both you and your children. For more information on grief issues, see books I've written on the subject at *www .sharonmarshallbooks.com.*

Problem Behaviors

Any major change in behavior that lasts longer than a fad or mood is a sign that our children are in crisis. Crises will not disappear without help. Stay close, ask questions, learn all you can about the kinds of pressure your children are facing.

If you see things that cause you to wonder whether they are involved in substance abuse, jump in. In these instances, don't be afraid of violating their privacy; addictions do not go away without help. If you were wrong, you can apologize. If you are right, your intrusion may save their lives.

I have given all students in my program permission to blame me for making healthy choices: "That Mrs. Lockett. She's making me go to afterschool tutoring!" Any time they need help saying "no" to unhealthy behaviors, I'm proud to be the bad guy.

·················· **REFLECTION** ··················

It wasn't boredom that taught me about win-win and personal responsibility; it was negativity. I had a conference period one year with a teacher who spent an hour each day telling me how terrible and stupid the students were. There aren't very many teachers like him. You know, those teachers who retired a few years ago and forgot to tell us, so we still send them students and give them a paycheck? There aren't many, but those few can make life miserable for both students and coworkers.

I spent the first three months that year either trying to talk him into loving students or trying to ignore him. Neither worked. Instead, he was draining me of energy. Finally, I realized that changing his mind wasn't my responsibility; changing my behavior and reactions was.

I looked for something we could agree on and found he was a gourmet chef. The rest of the year we traded recipes. Some of my favorite dishes today came from him.

19

I Study, but Fail the Test

"I work with my daughter. We study together. She knows the material, but she does poorly on the tests. I'm afraid if we don't get help soon, she'll quit trying. What can I do?"

Never give up! There are strategies you can try. If they don't work, there are specialists. Your daughter can succeed!

Juan's mother helped him with math homework every night. Juan knew how to do the math problems. He worked them correctly; she checked his work; she quizzed him; she did everything she needed to do to help Juan pass his math test. However, on Friday, Juan came home with an F. This went on for several weeks before Juan's mother finally approached the teacher to ask, "What can I do? How can I help Juan?"

The teacher pulled out Juan's exam papers for his mother to study. When she looked at the paper, she discovered that Juan had, indeed, worked every math problem correctly. He had to transfer the answer onto an answer sheet. He had transferred the answers to the wrong line.

In Juan's case, the culprit was an eye-hand coordination problem. Yes, Juan's teacher should have discovered that the problem wasn't mathematical. But Juan's teacher has between thirty and 200 students to analyze. Juan's mother is only concerned with one. Sometimes, we parents need to help out teachers.

191

Tell Them They're Smart

Jeff was in seventh grade before we finally found the right eye doctor. We had him tested; he got his glasses and started vision therapy. Because of my background, I worried about whether or not he would wear the glasses; I thought of the teasing he would have to endure.

As we drove home, I asked him if he was concerned about wearing the glasses. His response?

"Oh, no, Mom. I thought I was stupid."

I can't count the number of times I tried to validate Jeff's intelligence as we struggled to find what was causing him to fail an exam. But it doesn't matter; our children are smart enough to know that something is wrong when they study and fail. When all their efforts fail, they conclude that they are "stupid." Actually, "stupid" is a mild word for what they feel.

Over and over, we must tell them they are smart. But that is not enough. When we say, "You are smart," they get a spark of hope. If you stop with that statement, you can watch their eyes and see the light go out as the negative voices begin to play in their heads. You can actually watch hope die.

Say it anyway; but when you do, you must be specific and find something from their past to praise: "Remember how you knew just what to do when our puppy got hurt? That's smart; I didn't know what to do"; "Remember how you beat Uncle Moe when you played one-on-one basketball? That's smart. You actually outwitted him."

Then you say, "You have the answers right there in your brain. We're going to find a way to get them out."

Build Their Self-Esteem

I like the three-prong definition of self-esteem: Our sense of competence, our sense of belonging, and our sense of worth.

When children struggle to learn, their sense of competence is in jeopardy. We need to verbalize what we see them doing well. When they struggle to learn, we may want to ask for their help with our chores and tell them how valuable they are to us. While we discover the learning problem, we help them see themselves as capable.

Remember to "Work the Circle"

As you seek to discover why your children fail their tests, remember the concept of "working the circle" from Chapter 4. Try something that might point to a physical problem, then something emotional, then spiritual, then intellectual. Then do it all again.

Physical

When Jeff had his eye exam, Dr. Klingsheim, our behavioral optometrist, brought me in and put me through those tests on which Jeff had scored subnormal. He gave me special glasses and had me trace Gumby. As I complied, I thought, "I have better things to do with my time than trace Gumby."

When I finished, he held up my paper and said, "Here's yours." Alongside it, he held up Jeff's and said, "Here's Jeff's."

Talk about an ah-ha moment! The glasses had us use one eye at a time, and Jeff's Gumby had a three-quarter-inch gap right down the middle.

Is there a mismatch between verbal performance and written performance for your child? A child who can carry on an intelligent conversation but fails tests often has an eye-hand coordination problem. A child who does well in mathematical word problems that require comprehension but does poorly on a comprehension exam may have an eye-hand coordination problem, an ear problem, or an allergy that is negatively impacting learning. If there is a mismatch, if something doesn't make sense, begin looking for a physical culprit.

Say, "Read this passage aloud for me." If they skip little words, teach them to silently mouth the words. If this works, you have found a root cause. If it doesn't, you have used a Band-Aid. (Remember, Band-Aids are good.)

Remember that learning is related to the entire physiology. Some of our "behavior problem" children have food allergies; some can't hear as they should; some have vision problems; some have nutritional deficiencies (a growing epidemic in America today); some are sleep deprived.

Physical problems often point to a need for medical help. Don't try to diagnose the problem; try to observe the behaviors: "Rubs eyes; blinks; twitches; loses place reading, especially at night." Many ailments have the same symptoms. Your doctor can help lead you to the right source for help. Discuss these symptoms with your doctor, and do it again if you don't secure a resolution.

 Don't try to diagnose the problem; try to observe the behaviors.

Emotional

Because of Jeff's observed "abnormal behavior" in the classroom, I had him checked by a neurosurgeon, who suggested he was hyperactive and needed medication.

As I waited, I read his book that was on display in the waiting room. I discovered that emotional disorders have many of the same symptoms as hyperactivity. Jeff and I were recovering from a time of emotional turmoil; there had been four deaths and a divorce in our family over a period of thirteen months. One of the deaths was my infant son and Jeff's brother.

I'm not against medication, although I do think we are an overmedicated society. I just didn't believe it was the right intervention at the time. I chose, instead, to put Jeff in counseling. It was the right choice for us; we both got help with our grief and learned that one parent and one child do, indeed, make a family; not always the family of our choosing, but certainly the family of our heart.

Is your child a sensitive Phlegmatic personality? If so, your child may freeze if there is conflict in the classroom or if she senses that the teacher "doesn't like her." If this is the case, teach your child to compensate, to write out feelings, and to do some self-monitoring when she shuts down. If it is severe, you might register your child for a counseling session to learn how to "own her feelings" and talk them out—or for a class in assertive behavior. By all means, if this is the case, have a talk with your child's teacher. Teachers are eager to find a way to reach every child in the classroom. They will welcome your insights.

If your child is Sanguine, remember that Sanguine children do not respond to correction; they only respond to praise. Find out if they feel that the teacher is overly critical. If so, help your child to self-monitor reactions and work with the teacher on praise, rather than criticism, as the only effective strategy for motivating a Sanguine child.

 One parent and one child do, indeed, make a family; not always the family of our choosing, but certainly the family of our heart.

If your child is athletic, the mood of the game can cause an emotional high or an emotional low. During these times, they are periodically carried away into their own thoughts. In SCORE, we call this "going on vacation in class." In his book *Achieving Competitive Excellence*, Sports and Clinical Psychologist Ty Colbert describes the process as "dissociation": while our children sit in class, in their minds they replay a great sports achievement and celebrate—or an error they made and berate themselves. They look like they are listening, but they are a million miles away from what the teacher is saying. Revisiting the communication skills in Chapter 14 will help this child manage thoughts.

Sadly, we cannot overlook dysfunction. If there is or has been dysfunction in your family in any form (substance abuse, alcohol abuse, physical abuse, verbal abuse—even a family illness that causes the child to take on adult responsibilities), it will impact learning. There is good news, though; help is available. It's time to break the cycle. Your doctor can lead you to the right agency or support group. Twelve-step programs are springing up all across the nation to help us deal with every level of dysfunction, and they're free.

Twelve-Step Programs

To find a twelve-step program that is right for you and your children, consult community directories or visit one of the following Web sites:
- *www.alcoholics-anonymous.org*
- *www.12step.org*
- *www.christianrecovery.org*
- *www.notalone.org*

Anything that "hurts the heart" is cause to grieve. A child five months old shows visible signs of grief with the loss of a parent or significant caretaker. These events happen in life, but thinking that a child is unaffected by them is a myth. If your heart has been broken for any reason, remember your children as you grieve and rebuild.

Spiritual

I had a young man once tell me that his parents lied to him all the time. As I listened to what he had to say, I discovered that his parents had recently divorced. His mother told her side of the story; his father told his. The stories did not agree, so the child concluded that both parents were lying—the very parents who had taught him to always tell the truth.

Although we think of divorce in the family as an emotional issue, it causes a spiritual battle in your children because something is happening that goes against their family values. Keep in mind that relationships in the home can undermine learning.

When one child is abusing drugs or involved in something that compromises values, an entire family is affected. If substance abuse is in your home, even by another family member, your child's learning capacity can be compromised.

Dreams die hard. If your child wanted to be an airline pilot and suddenly needs glasses, it will cause a "spiritual" battle. Help him grieve; then help him dream again. When their hearts are broken, our children can't see that there will ever be a new dream.

Intellectual

When we evaluated SCORE, we measured the amount of time students spent doing homework and studying. We thought, through our activities, that we would motivate them to spend longer hours on homework. We found that the amount of time they spent did not change. However, they were turning in homework more often, using better study strategies, and earning higher grades. They were studying "smart."

Does your child perform better on objective tests than on essay exams? Or is the reverse true? I can fail an objective test and make an A on an essay exam on the same day over the same material. I naturally learn in concepts rather than details. I can read something and have an emotional attachment to it, but not remember the names. If this is the case with your children, studying with friends who learn differently will help raise that test grade.

Take advantage of the theory of multiple intelligences (Chapter 5). Work from your child's intuitive strength; then go back to help make sense of classroom material.

Root Cause

Any number of things can account for understanding material but failing tests, but there is always a root cause. The cause is always rooted in the physical, emotional, spiritual, or intellectual beings. The problem is finding the root; until you do, everything you try will be a Band-Aid. Band-Aids are good, they are sometimes necessary, but they are not enough. When you discover the root, you can find a resolution.

If you can't help your child break through the anxiety after a few attempts, it is time to seek outside help. See Chapter 23.

Help with Test Anxiety

The first time I became aware of the severity of test anxiety, I was teaching a business class. I reviewed for a test, and Rebecca raised her hand enthusiastically for every answer. Every time I called on her, she was right. She did her homework and understood the concepts. I gave the test, graded it that night, and she had failed. The next day, I verbally retested her to check her comprehension. After validating the fact she knew the material, I asked what happened. She said, "Oh, I always fail tests! I just get so nervous!"

Rebecca's problem was bigger than my expertise at the time. I referred her for counseling. In the meantime, I gave her an oral exam either just before or just after the test without her knowing she was being tested. I averaged her A on the oral exam with the F on the written exam to give her a C on that test. Since her class work was always A, she ended up with at least a B as her overall class grade.

Is this fair to the students who studied and mastered the exam? As fair as it is to allow the student who doesn't study but can crack an exam to earn the A. In hindsight, I wish I had done more for her.

Often very bright students freeze on a test. If you suspect test anxiety, begin studying "whole brain."

We have both a short-term and a long-term memory system. Our long-term memory bank stores an incredible amount of information—everything we have ever learned. The information is in the long-term memory; the problem is one of accessing the information.

To routinely retrieve it, that information needs to be understood at an application level and used periodically. We can easily memorize things by drill and practice; but to readily access them, they need to have meaning to us. Again, using the example of computer terminology, we know it's in there, but we forgot what we named the file.

When our children "forget the file name," having them add a dimension to it will trigger their memory. For example, if they draw a picture (in computer terminology, create an icon), sing a song, or rhythmically move, they have created a mnemonic device that will help them remember. Mnemonic devices serve as right-brain triggers into the left-brain memory bank. They retrieve the information that is stored in long-term memory and enable us to express it differently, using movement, song, dance, music, art . . . the list is endless.

- Sing the information to the tune of a song you know. Remember the theories (sets of three, etc.; see Chapters 11 and 20). Try times tables to "London Bridge Is Falling Down": *Six times three is eighteen; six times three is eighteen. Six times three is eighteen. Eighteen.*
- Dance six times three: Dance six pirouettes each in three different rooms of the house. How many pirouettes did you make?
- Use visual imagery: Imagine six little boys eating six smart sandwiches and drinking six glasses of brain milk, and, poof, each boy grows two more heads. How many heads are there now?
- Draw out those same times tables: six lines containing three stars each:

*	*	*
*	*	*
*	*	*
*	*	*
*	*	*
*	*	*

Remember "Divide and Conquer"

I once worked with a group of approximately 100 middle school students who were failing at least one class. That failure could cause them not to graduate. It was three weeks until the end of school. They each had to pass at least one exam.

I divided them by the class they were failing: English, history, math, science. Their first task was, as a group, to identify what they needed to learn. After a few minutes of discussion, every group responded with behaviors rather than content:

We have to listen in class.

We have to take notes in class.

We have to attend class regularly.

I said, "This is the emergency room! You don't have time to just listen. You have to study. What will be on that test?"

They didn't know. They knew behaviors, but not what content was important.

When our children study for hours but don't retain much, it is often because they keep going over the same material, usually without a focus. Most of it they already know so they are simply reviewing rather than learning new information.

Name It

Have them identify what they are supposed to study. They need to know the specifics—e.g., "The test will cover the concepts in Chapter 7 of my fourth grade math book. It will consist of ten double-digit multiplication problems, and ten double-digit division problems." With that information, you know to have them study three ways (review Chapters 11 and 20):

1. What math facts do they need to study? Use the flash cards to "divide and conquer." Study only those they don't know, in sets of three, for five to fifteen minutes. Set them aside for at least two hours; divide and conquer again; study again, in sets of three, for five to fifteen minutes.
2. Do they know how to do double-digit multiplication? Have them work three sample problems. If they know how to

do them, they don't need to study double-digit multiplication. If they don't know how to do them, have them "teach you" all the steps of the sample problems. Continue to add problems until they "get it right three times."

3. Do they know how to do double-digit division? Have them work three sample problems. If they know how to do them, they don't need to study double-digit division. If they don't know how to do them, have them "teach you" all the steps of the sample problems. Continue to add problems until they "get it right three times."

Identify What They Don't Know

If they have taken class or reading notes using predicted test questions, memory keys, or pictures, they can use those notes to study. Cover up the notes and review the questions. If they know the answer, they move on; they don't need to study. If they don't remember, they study—again, using the theories.

Study Smart

In sets of three, drill *only on the information they do not know.* Remember their best modality; remember their best intelligence. Study from their point of strength.

Never Quit

The only ultimate failure in life is falling down one time more than you get up.

.... **REFLECTION** ....

When Harvey Williams was nine years old, he and his family were accosted by members of the Ku Klux Klan. They fled in the middle of the night, with horse and buggy carrying all their earthly possessions.

At age thirteen, Harvey Williams started school and flunked algebra—three times!

Today, Harvey Williams holds three PhDs. He is retired from his position as Director of Admissions for the College of Medicine at the University of California–Irvine.

I once asked Harvey, "When do you tell students they're not going to make it?"

He replied, "You never have that right. You tell them what they have to do. The choice is always theirs."

Harvey is one of few people I know whose past could cause him to hate me just because of the color of my skin, but Harvey doesn't seem to have a hate bone in his body. He truly "got up one time more than he fell down."

20

I Understood It in Class

"I find my daughter just staring at a blank paper. When I ask what's wrong, she says she doesn't know how to do the work. Usually I scold her for not asking questions in class, and she solemnly declares, 'I understood it in class, so I didn't have any questions!' Help!"

Having listened to students for years, I am convinced of one thing: they really do think they understand it in class. Then they come home to do homework and draw a blank! There they sit, staring at a problem, not knowing where to begin. The longer they sit, the more convinced they become that they are incapable of learning (*stupid* is the word they use when we're getting acquainted; after they know me, they realize I won't let them use that word).

How do we help them?

Ask the "What Happened?" Questions

Sometimes this blanking out is the result of simple anxiety. They don't understand an early question, so they freeze. Encourage them to skip to a problem they can do. If skipping is hard for them, have them write, "I don't know how to do this," and leave a blank space for each question they need to skip. When they find one they can do, their confidence returns. Once they complete a few problems, they gain confidence and refresh their memory. Then they can go back to fill in the blanks.

Sometimes they blank out because they were relying on the book or board examples in class but didn't really comprehend the concepts. Having them take class notes will help; they are far more likely to remember concepts if they have written them rather than just listening in class. If they do this but don't remember, help them create a series of questions to ask their teacher the next day. Often this process alone will jog their memory. If not, it will at least impress their teacher!

Sometimes students blank out because, even though they have the information stored in their long-term memory, they've forgotten how to access it. When this is the case, have them use right-brain strategies:

- Draw a picture of what they think the question is asking.
- Put it into a song.
- Make an absurd association.
- Talk it out with you.
- Act out the question.
- Turn the question into a baseball game or a chess tournament.

A right-brain technique often triggers memory and allows them to retrieve the information.

In our SCORE classrooms we always have students express things two ways, both in words and using symbols, visuals, songs, dance, or rap. They're constantly going from right-brain to left-brain, learning with what we call a whole-brain experience.

Reach Out

No matter what the problem, you're not alone in helping your child come to a solution. Here are some outside resources to seek out when you're stuck.

Call a Friend

Often, if your child is confused, so are his classmates. Have your child keep a phone list for each class in his notebook. When he gets stuck, he can call a friend. They can talk it out on the phone, then hang up and finish their work. If neither of them understands it, they are more willing to ask questions in class; there is security in numbers.

Check Out Tutoring

If the school offers a tutorial or an afterschool study class, have your child attend it two or three times a week. Sometimes teachers stay in their classrooms certain days of the week so students who need help can drop in. Some schools schedule students into a SCORE class to help them understand and master content. If they take advantage of these resources, their questions can be answered on the spot; and they will learn more if they discuss it with peers. If the school doesn't offer a tutorial, suggest they start one.

Call a Hotline

If the school offers a homework hotline, keep the number handy—and keep the teachers who answer it busy! Schools or communities with a homework hotline pay a teacher to sit at a phone through the evening, just to answer homework questions. The teacher gets paid for sitting if the phone doesn't ring. Don't let that happen with your tax money!

See What the Internet Has to Offer

You can search "help with homework" and look for an appropriate site. This is a growing field. Currently, most sites are free. Don't get locked into an expensive subscription fee without doing some research on what is available and how easy it is to use.

Consider Hiring a Tutor

Especially if your children struggle in the area of reading or math, consider hiring someone to work with them to make sure homework is completed and that they comprehend the content. That way, you'll be validated by an outside person if you need to speak to a school authority or a teacher.

Try Doing the Problem Yourself

When children struggle to the point of frustration, they become emotionally committed to failure (see Chapter 21). Once they reach that point, it is especially difficult to help them. Intervene, then, before they get to that place.

Ask your child what he has tried. After he has tried to solve the problem or answer the question for a few minutes, you try it. If it is obvious to you what to do, help him with what to do first. Once he understands, you can leave him to work. Come back to check on him; then help him know what to do next. This way, you are breaking it into bite-sized pieces for him.

If you can't work it either, have him write, "I don't know how to do this" on his paper. You sign it, verifying to the teacher that your child made the effort. Teachers don't know when homework is difficult unless children and their parents communicate it to them.

Remind Them of Their Successes

The most important thing we can do as parents is to validate our children's intellectual ability when they draw a blank. The longer they struggle, the more they become emotionally committed to failure. You need to point out how smart they are by reminding them of their past success.

 The longer they struggle, the more they become emotionally committed to failure.

················ **REFLECTION** ·················

Shortly after immigrating with his family from Mexico, Rigo Chacon started kindergarten in a school that punished students for speaking any language other than English. As a result, many of his primary school memories are those of being forced to keep quiet or, more often, being punished for speaking.

When Rigo was in sixth grade, he demonstrated his command of English by winning his local spelling bee. Before the news could be made formal, he was required to repeat the competition "to prove he had won." In anger over this unfair situation, Rigo learned a great lesson from his father: the strength of human dignity. He knew he had won, the school officials knew he had won, the girl he was competing against knew he had won. He would compete again, even though it was unfair. Rigo learned the power of succeeding, regardless of the circumstance, by working within a faulty system instead of against it. He won the second time around and went on to be the first Hispanic representative from his local school in national competition.

When Rigo moved to California, he developed his exceptional speaking talent into an art form. A speech teacher at San Jose High School recruited him for the debate team—a team that went on to win national honors.

Rigo Chacon recently retired from his position as news anchor-man for Channel 7 News in San Jose, California. He excelled in a competitive and rigorous field, utilizing his talent in speech and knowledge of Spanish for the public's benefit. He is a reminder to all of us that we can succeed with dignity, regardless of our circumstances.

21

I Can Never Learn It—Never!

"I don't know what to do with him. He says he can't do his work so I try to help him, and he won't cooperate. No wonder he's struggling. He won't even try."

This describes the students we call "emotionally committed to failure." They would rather look belligerent than stupid so they quit trying. But read on! There is help available.

When Mr. Jones gave his first test of the year, one of his students, toward the beginning of the test, threw his pen down, slumped in his chair, and said a few choice words. Mr. Jones walked up to him and asked what was going on. The student said, "Your test sucks."

Mr. Jones had just finished teaching SCORE's Communications unit. He said to his student, "We learned about feedback in here, and I don't know what 'sucks' means. Tell me what's wrong with the test?"

The young man identified two terms in test question two that he did not understand. Mr. Jones explained those two terms. The student sat up, finished his test, and earned a B on it.

He moved from an F to a B on a test because we, as teachers, have learned to use feedback to keep students from continuing their emotional commitment to failure.

Deal with Their Emotional Commitment to Failure

When your child says, "I can never learn it," in one of its many forms (e.g., "the test sucks"), she is emotionally committed to failure. When a student has tried and failed, tried and failed, tried and failed, after a period of time even a young child will think (subconsciously), "I would rather look stubborn than stupid." They will cop an attitude and say, "I just don't care any more."

The emotional commitment to failure needs to be dealt with before you can effectively access study techniques. First, remind them of past, related success:

"Yes, you can learn how to work word problems. Remember when we played Ad Libs? And Charades? You know how Uncle Andy is always asking you those funny questions where you have to think to answer? Those are a little like word problems."

Next, tell them what you expect. "When students know precisely what is expected of them, they tend to adjust their behavior to receive the reward and avoid the punishment" (see SCORE Learning Theory 7, Appendix A). They need to know that there is no "wiggle room;" otherwise, they will play games trying to get out of the task:

"You will do the word problems; I'd like to help you."

But everyone needs a choice!

"Will you let me help?"

Once that offer is made, we must give them the freedom to pout for a while if they would like. It is, after all, their choice. Once they agree to your help, give them the parameters:

"First you tell me what you've been thinking while you tried to work this problem, then you and I will discuss it to see if we can come up with a solution together. If we spend 10 minutes on this problem and neither of us can figure it out, we'll decide it's a stinky one and we'll set it aside. I'll write your teacher a note."

Or *"Let's skip this problem and go to the next one. Maybe after we figure out the next one, it will make this one easier."*

Or *"I am setting the kitchen timer for five minutes. After you've tried for five minutes on your own, I'll sit down and help you out."*

Early, they need a reward:

"As soon as you either finish this or spend fifteen minutes on it, we'll take a break. We can play catch for ten minutes, and then we'll come back to homework."

You reward your child for putting in the time, completing an assignment, or doing a job well based on what he or she would need as a reward. The following are common examples:

- A television program
- Playing catch for ten minutes
- Calling a friend
- Listening to three songs
- Jogging around the block
- Text-messaging a friend
- Going online

The rewards are endless. The important thing is that they should mean something to the child involved. One of my after-school programs uses this technique. The students at the high school are into "Theatro." The director, knowing they want to participate in a drama group that travels, set that up as their reward. Their ticket to Theatro practice in the afternoon is having spent one hour in tutoring. They are making amazing gains academically and enjoying themselves while they're at it.

Get Them Through the Crisis

When your child says, "I can't learn," he needs some TLC. You need to sit down beside him and ask questions: "What do you think you would do next?" "Let's see if we can find that word in what you're reading."

Walk through the process of solving the problem with him. Don't do the work for him, but sit beside him and hold his hand.

When he is "willing but unable," he needs you to participate in the process of homework. Don't cook dinner while you talk to him from the kitchen; literally sit down beside him. When he comes to a point where he knows what to do next (we call it an ah-ha moment), you can leave him for a few moments to do it on his own. Check back with him in a few minutes. Make sure that when he's done it well you celebrate with him. Pat him on the back, reward him in some way, and let him know you're proud of him. When he's reached the point of not believing in himself, he needs this intensive kind of encouragement.

Once children have gone beyond the feelings of failure to having a bad attitude, the intervention needs to be a bit more straightforward. In this case, the child needs to be told, "This is what you do next. Do it." Be firm. Monitor while it's done. Even if she's angry, she gets it done. Say, again, "This is what you do next; do it now."

At this stage, your child may use words you never taught her and wish she didn't know. She may be angry. She may give you the old "Whatever!" with a sigh. She may say things she will deeply regret some day when she has children of her own. But success breeds success. Once she starts achieving, she will be back to normal.

Stay in close touch with her until you get through the crisis and she again becomes a willing learner.

Of course, you probably know that I don't believe there is any such thing as a child who can't do the work, so this "emotional commitment to failure" isn't that they can't do the work, but that they don't believe they can do the work. Even though you know they can, when they're expressing "I can't," you need to be their partner in leading them through.

Remember: You're the Leader

As a parent, you are the leader in your home. You may feel as though you are a dethroned leader; you may be a disenchanted leader; you may even be an inadequate leader. But you do head your home. In your role, you will want to develop your leadership skills.

 We need to lead the way our children need to be led.

Ken Blanchard first got me excited about the topic of "Situational Leadership." It has become revolutionary in both my personal life and in the SCORE program. You must read his books, especially *Leadership and the One-Minute Manager: Increasing Effectiveness Through Situational Leadership*; my "nutshell" version is this: We need to lead the way our children need to be led.

When our children are "willing and able," we need to let them do it and praise them often. If we interfere, they may shut down.

When our children are "willing but unable," we need to sit down with them and hold their hands. We need to help them discover what to do next. We need to check back with them and guide them to the next step.

When our children are "unwilling but able," they need some fun. We need to tease them, laugh with them, play games with them . . . but not let them off the hook.

When our children are "unwilling and unable," we need to be directive: "Do this, this way, by this time." When they comply (after their griping has ended), validate them and help them discover the next step.

Our children are so funny in the aftermath of these loving encounters. My observation has been that I feel terrible when I have to give orders. I worry that I was too tough. I actually lose sleep over whether or not I could have handled it better. They never tell me thanks when they succeed. However, I often hear them bragging to a friend about what they accomplished during those times.

You just have to read the Blanchard book!

Use the Learning Principles

The more I listen to students talk about school, the more I am convinced that most students study and attempt to do well in their classes. The problem is that they work "hard" rather than "smart" as they endeavor to learn. The "smart" learner knows how to apply some tested strategies; thus retention is enhanced, and real learning occurs in a shorter period of time.

To learn "smart," they need only apply a unique combination of the following fifteen techniques. Does that seem too simple? It really isn't, for it will take us each a lifetime to learn how to creatively apply these principles. I'm still learning new approaches after more than thirty years in education.

1. If you say and/or write a fact over and over again, you will put it in your memory very firmly. This does not mean just reading something several times; it means saying it and/or writing it multiple times. But beware: See number two!

2. When memorizing facts, material becomes rote after the third repetition. Therefore, rotate material to be memorized in sets of three repetitions. Something occurs in our brain after about the third repetition—we "shift into neutral" and cease to process new information. Once we cease to think as we study, we could repeat something 100 times without substantially increasing our retention. Give new information three repetitions, and then move on. Give that same information three more repetitions next time it rotates to the top of your stack of flash cards.

3. Optimum time for memorization is five to fifteen minutes at intervals of two to twenty-four hours. When we concentrate at the level necessary for memory, we tire our brain after about fifteen minutes (this is "drill and practice," not comprehension or application). We need to wait at least two hours before we repeat the process to allow our brain to rest, but no more than twenty-four hours or we forget too much and must relearn the material rather than review it. The best way to cram for an exam is to study hard for fifteen minutes, sleep for two hours, and study hard for another fifteen minutes, all night long (unless, of course, you have a habit of ignoring alarm clocks, as I do!).

4. The more senses that are involved in the learning process, the more rapidly learning will occur. If we just read information quietly, we are likely to forget 90 percent of it. If we read aloud, we have added our senses of speech and hearing to our sense of sight, and we should remember at least 30 percent with the same investment of time. Some sources say we retain 50 percent because combining senses has an expanding effect, unless something in the oral or written process distracts us. Students who worry about pronouncing words correctly may learn to read well orally, for example, but have lower comprehension rates when they do so, because they are focusing their energy on sounding good rather than understanding. We can add our senses of smell and taste to the learning process through visual imagery. For example, imagine the smell and taste of freshly baked bread while you read a story that includes a descriptive passage of walking through the town square.

5. Study a few items at a time. This is another way of saying "divide and conquer." Often we frustrate ourselves in the learning process by studying too much material at one time. We should limit our new material to between fifteen and twenty-five items, or we might review twenty items and add five new ones during a study session.

6. Study only what you don't know. Students often spend hours studying from a textbook, but most of their time is spent reviewing what they already know rather than studying what they don't know. Instead, review by dividing material to be learned into two stacks: that which you already know, and that which you need to study. Spend your five to fifteen minutes on what you don't know. Wait two to twenty-four hours; mix the material up, and divide it again. You will find you have forgotten some old material and learned some new material. You now have a new five-to-fifteen minute stack to study.

7. When students know what to expect, they are likely to adjust their behavior to receive the reward and avoid problems. Well . . .

there are exceptions. But most students, most of the time, will do what they know is expected of them. And most students will test those expectations and play the odds. If homework is not negotiable and is consistently checked, most students will give in and get it done. The same is true for quality. Some personalities are perfectionistic; others need to have a parental quality check at regular intervals.

8. If you ask yourself a question to which the new information is the right answer, then say the fact to yourself as the answer, you will increase your memory capability. This technique is especially effective with reading comprehension. Create a question and/or read the questions at the end of the chapter before you begin to read. This alerts you about what to watch for and helps you know what the author considers important.

9. It is easier to remember information if it is associated with something you already know. Alphabetizing, sequencing, and categorizing make learning easier. Singing information to the tune of a song you know well makes learning easier.

10. If you set up categories before beginning to read, it is easier to notice things that fit into the categories, thus easier to remember the new information. Kindergartners divide picture cards into animal, vegetable, and mineral. If we were studying a war, categories might be: factors leading up to the war, strategies used during the war, negotiating the war's end, and restoring diplomacy.

11. It is easier to remember new information if you make an absurd association. The more absurd the association, the more likely it will stick in memory. Associations become absurd when we exaggerate proportions or give animate characteristics to inanimate objects (e.g., imagine walking by a daisy and having it wink). You can give the math problems a shape and draw a picture of the problem you are trying to solve. And yes, information can go into long-term memory this way, just as it can using the other theories.

12. If material is personalized, it is remembered longer. This technique can work in a variety of ways. You can substitute your children's names for characters in a story. Relating a math problem to a child's allowance personalizes material. Transferring something learned to an everyday event makes material personal.

13. A student will learn material more thoroughly if asked to explain it to someone else. The teacher always learns far more than the student, because material has to be thoroughly learned in order to explain it to another person. So switch roles! You become the student and let your child become the teacher. This works even when you don't understand the content, and it can be done in a different language (see Chapter 1).

14. It is best to schedule your studying so you don't study similar subjects in sequence. Reading comprehension and mathematical calculations both utilize the entire brain, but activity is most concentrated in different parts. A heavy study schedule is easier to get through if you rest one part of your brain a little while you concentrate activities in another.

15. Students will tend to study more effectively and avoid burnout if they build refreshing and rewarding breaks into their study period. A reward for one child might be a phone call to a friend; for another, it might be a television program; for yet another, it might be a vigorous swim. Let children select their own rewards, but give them a break.

In addition to these basic learning theories, perhaps a reminder about food is in order. A hungry child cannot learn efficiently; low blood sugar impairs the short-term memory. A child on a sugar high cannot learn efficiently; high blood sugar impairs the short-term memory and compromises the attention span. Keep a supply of nutritious snacks near your study area (cookies are okay if accompanied by milk or another protein), and never insist that your child finish homework before he can eat.

· · · · · · · · · · · · · · · **REFLECTION** · · · · · · · · · · · · · · · ·

Mr. Gomez was counselor to potential dropouts at his high school. Often he sat in the midst of parent/child conflict. One mother and son especially stood out: they came in angry at one another. As the three of them walked down the hallway, Mr. Gomez listened to the dialogue:

Mother: "You never tell me where you're going."

Son: "You're always on my case."

And so it continued, the yammering. As they entered the office, Mr. Gomez turned to the mother after her yelling, "I worry about you when you don't come home," and said, simply, "You really love him, don't you."

They left arm in arm.

In the midst of our struggles to maintain the daily routine, let's not forget the language of love and how powerful it is.

22

I Don't Have Any Homework

"He never has any homework. And most of the time I really don't think he does! What's wrong with education that one child has more than he can possibly accomplish, and the other one has nothing!? And how do I handle it and be both fair and consistent?"

Sometimes this is a true statement; sometimes it is a power struggle between children and their parents or teachers. Often this power struggle goes on with a bright child, certainly capable of finishing work in class, but often involved in a battle for control, with homework as a weapon.

What to Do

Even when this statement reflects a power struggle, even when one child doesn't have homework but another has too much, there are steps to success. Try any or all of the following:

Reduce the Battle!

Make homework non-negotiable. Make every night a homework night. This is designed around the theory that when students know what is expected of them, they will usually adjust their behavior to receive the reward and avoid the punishment.

Read

Set aside time each school night for reading or homework. Research suggests that those who read will become good readers (research is sometimes so mundane!). I suggest fifteen minutes to one hour of leisure reading, depending on the age of the child. Include a comprehension check on nights when there is no homework.

Include You!

Take time from your much-too-busy schedule to read for leisure.

Join In

Read a good family story, alternating readers, for a family bonding experience. You'll likely find you enjoy your childhood reading more the second time through than you did as a child.

Communicate

Keep communication open with your child's teacher. Be sure you know the school's phone number, the teacher's e-mail address and conference period, and when you can reach the school staff. My general observation is that most teachers are better at responding to e-mail than they are at returning phone calls. Many teachers now post homework assignments on a Web page so parents can check them.

Check Assignments

Remember to check the calendar and assignment sheet (Chapter 13). That way you have a checklist. You can also help your child plan ahead for projects and book reports.

Check Notes

Check class notes every day. If they're not done, homework is to re-create them.

Take Breaks

Remember the theory "Build refreshing and rewarding breaks." Sometimes when all the homework is done, take an evening off. Do something that is just plain old fun with the entire family.

Managing Power Struggles

Jeff is Phlegmatic so I had to teach him to stand up for himself and express his viewpoints. Unfortunately, I taught him too well.

We were arguing loudly over something—I don't remember what. He got louder; I got louder. Finally, I stopped.

I said, "Jeff! I don't know why we're fighting over this. I want you to win."

"Humph!," he said. "It sure doesn't feel like it."

I replied, "You can make this decision. I just want you to think it through. I want to be heard. Then I'll honor whatever you decide to do. I'm your mother. I want more in life for you than I do for me. I will *always* be on your side."

If you discover that the no-homework issue is actually a power struggle (in other words, your child has homework but is having a battle over whether or not to do it), you want to get to the root of the power struggle. Sometimes it is the child saying, "I want you to treat me like an adult." In fact, let's face it: some of our children were born grown-ups. If that's the case, you might need to let him assume that responsibility, which may mean taking a lower grade.

If the power struggle is with the teacher, you may need to schedule a conference. You may simply need to look at personality dynamics and help your child understand how to "give the teacher what she needs in order to get what you want." See Chapters 6 through 9 and my book *Smarter, Not Harder!*

If a power struggle is actually your child acting out some dysfunction at school or at home, you want to help the child realize that that is what we call "stinkin' thinkin'." Help your child learn skills that will enable them to negotiate life's difficult situations.

If this is going on because the child truly has no homework, you might want to talk with the teacher. You might also want to talk with the teacher if your other child has too much homework. There should be a balance, but every teacher and every child is different.

The most creative excuse I ever received as a teacher for having missed homework was "My little brother flushed it down the toilet." I laughed. It was an eight-page bound report. I said, "Well, I wouldn't want your plumbing bill."

REFLECTION

In a summer program, we had our students divided in small groups among groups of teachers who were also in a summer workshop. Nine of our ten groups went like clockwork. In the tenth group, the teachers didn't take the assignment seriously and did an inferior job.

Initially, the students were pleased, because it got them out of having to do work. In the dorms each evening, however, they talked to their peers. By Thursday, they were livid. They came to me with comments such as, "Those teachers just don't care. They don't like us. They're doing this on purpose. The others are learning and doing fun things. We're being cheated."

I offered to go to the teachers with them, but they didn't want me to intervene. Instead, that evening, for their homework, we sat down together and designed a plan of action whereby the students would confront the teachers in class the next day. We taught them about feedback. We taught them about building a bridge, not a wall or a war. We helped them formulate statements that were "I" statements, not "you" statements.

The next day in class, they shared their feelings with the teachers:

"The other classes are doing really interesting assignments and learning a lot. I feel cheated because we didn't learn anything new."

"I feel angry, as though my time was wasted."

These students learned far more than the others did because they learned how to confront in a healthy way, and they learned how to take responsibility when things seemed unfair.

23

Where to Find Help

"But I've tried it all. I'll think we're making headway, but it's three steps forward, two steps back. I know he's bright, but I sincerely believe he's as frustrated as I am. I don't know what to do next."

Below you'll find some things to do when nothing can be done.

He was lauded as the "best pediatric neurosurgeon" in the area, and my son had been referred to him for hyperactivity. He discussed Jeff's "inappropriate" behavior—Jeff didn't stay in a little testing room, not much larger than a closet, with no windows and with the door closed. Jeff quickly (and not very neatly) completed his task and walked out to chat with the receptionist.

I responded that I had never locked Jeff in a closet, I didn't like being closed in either, and I was never good at drawing pictures.

"That doesn't make it right," he countered. He suggested that I might need medication, too.

Some children need medication for hyperactivity. Somewhere deep inside, I didn't believe it was the right solution at this time for Jeff. I chose not to follow his advice and not to put my son (or myself) on medication. I am thankful now, but I spent many insecure days agonizing over my decision. You see, he had managed to tap into my personal insecurities. That made me less able to help my son.

"But," you say, "I've tried to help, but they forget . . .
or fight me . . .
or try but don't succeed . . . . So
I feel insecure. I have done all I know to do. So
I wonder if *they* have a *problem.*
I hate myself for having those thoughts so
I shove them into my subconscious where they
fester and periodically erupt!
I've seen . . .
teachers,
friends,
doctors,
therapists.
I feel powerless. I am as frustrated as my children.
Where do I find help?"

You can tap into the resources of your child, the school, the medical community, libraries, the Internet, and elsewhere.

Your Child

I was running a summer live-in program for 100 high school students on a university campus. That evening, I was exhausted. As I left a counseling session in the dorm, I glanced at the sofa in the living room to find one of my girls, with head down, pouting. One of my team leaders was sitting beside her. I thought, "I'm glad he's got it covered; I'm too tired for another crisis."

As I started out the door, I glanced over my shoulder just as she looked up and caught my eye. I dropped everything, started running toward her, and yelled to anyone within earshot, "Call the medics!"

Waiting for the medics to arrive, I asked, "What did you take?"

"Tylenol," she drawled.

"This isn't about getting kicked out of the program now; this is life and death. What did you take?"

"Tylenol."

I repeated: "Tell me the truth. This is life and death. We have to know in order to help you."

It was Tylenol. She was having an allergic reaction. Reactions to Tylenol are rare, but they can be deadly.

We spent the night in the emergency room, and she was fine.

I know I had to ask, but I wish I had believed her sooner.

I almost feel trite writing this, but I will: Listen to—and believe—what your child has to say. He won't always know how to say it; she won't always make a fair assessment; he may not be tactful when he cries out for help—but they are usually honest when they make statements such as "Sometimes I can't see" and "I read it and thought I got it right, but then the teacher read it and I answered it wrong."

The School

Yes, the other half of Jeff's personality is Sanguine. He cried so seldom as a baby that one day we decided to take a picture of him while he was crying. The moment he saw the camera flash, he smiled!

Then along came school. His first-grade teacher worried about him because he wouldn't sit still to do his work, so we had him observed by the school psychologist. We both had a good laugh when she gave me her report.

He spotted her observing him so he started a conversation (Sanguines talk to anyone who will listen). When she left him to observe another child in the class, he followed her—her work looked far more interesting than his!

If your child is having trouble at school, your first source of help is the classroom teacher. Ask for advice; ask for strategies; ask what help the school offers; ask for referrals. If this isn't fruitful, go to the counselor; then the principal; then the district superintendent; then the school board.

The school nurse should be able to provide first-line screening for visual, auditory, and nutritional disorders that are affecting schoolwork. If something is discovered, she can provide you with referrals for finding a solution.

The school psychologist can help you with first-line screening for psychological and/or psychomotor disorders. If something is discovered, he can provide you with referrals for finding a solution.

Ask your school if they offer tutorials and, if so, make sure your child attends them. Tutorials are manned by either trained tutors or teachers who are paid to help students who are struggling with content or with homework. If the school offers a tutorial, the tutorial is usually free to you, the parent. One of my schools sends notices out with progress reports. They say, "Feed 'em when they're hungry."

Make sure you know the e-mail addresses and the preparation periods of your child's teachers. That way, you can call or e-mail when you need help on a concept or with assignments. Also, check out your school's Web page. Often teachers will post homework assignments on the Web and provide little pointers for completing assignments.

See if your school offers a homework hotline. If so, make sure you know the phone number. A teacher is there to answer questions that children have on all subjects, at all grade levels. Take advantage of this when your child struggles with homework.

Check out the following Web resources:

www.free.ed.gov
www.aleks.com
http://school.discovery.com/homeworkhelp/bjpinchbeck
www.refdesk.com/homework.html
www.cainelearning.com

The Medical Community

My son had vision problems that we didn't discover until seventh grade (you read about them earlier). When I told his pediatrician I had him in vision therapy, the pediatrician said to me, "Well, you just wasted your money." I laughed and said, "I've wasted a lot of money, but never for anything better than this."

The medical community is divided over the issue of vision therapy, and there is certainly a charlatan in every profession. I happened to have found a good behavioral optometrist. He kept telling me exactly what he was doing, and it has made a major difference throughout Jeff's entire life. Inside, I knew it was right when we found him. Even though I didn't know what else to do, that little voice inside told me that the ophthalmologist was wrong when he discounted Jeff's comment, "Sometimes I can't see." In other words, "trust your gut."

Some days later, I visited my ophthalmologist who had a daughter Jeff's age. She asked how Jeff was doing, and I laughed and said, "You're not going to approve of this, but I just placed him in vision therapy." Her comment was "Don't judge me; tell me how it played out." When I explained to her what they had done with Jeff and how his school work had improved, she said, "You were in the right place, and you found a good doctor. Sometimes when I have children that I can't help, I refer them to vision therapy; but I ask them to be very careful, because there are vision specialists out there who keep you paying them forever without significant results."

Discuss your concerns with your pediatrician, asking for a referral if necessary. Those who typically deal with learning-related problems are behavioral optometrists and pediatric audiologists.

The following symptoms may indicate a vision, hearing, food allergy, or emotional problem:

- There is a discrepancy between verbal performance and written performance.
- They use a ruler to cover up content on a page, and slide the ruler down while reading. Children who do this may intuitively be compensating for a vision problem. Sometimes minor vision problems cause the eyes to jump from

one line to another, so they're actually compensating for the fact that their eyes move in a funny way.

- They read with the page turned at an angle or their heads turned.
- They are unable to sit still very long; they read for a few minutes and then are up around the room doing something else. This may indicate eye fatigue or eye strain. It may also be hyperactivity.
- They have behavioral problems at school—e.g., they're up wandering around the room, they're not paying attention, they're easily distracted. They may be compensating for the fact that they can't hear or their eyes aren't quite working right. Since the search for meaning is innate (according to brain research), they're actually up around the room disrupting people, searching for something that makes sense to them.
- There is a major change in your child's behavior either just before or just after meals. There may be a food allergy or a condition of some kind such as hypoglycemia or diabetes. These do affect learning.
- You notice that they frequently twitch and blink.

Does your child mispronounce some words? Children with mild hearing disorders often have trouble speaking. The letter R is especially difficult to pronounce. Your school can help you with referrals to a speech therapist.

As you work with the medical community, let me urge you not to be intimidated. Ask your deepest questions, express your greatest fears. Know that the medical community is limited to the information that you give them. Tell them everything you observe, even if you don't think it is relevant; they base their judgments on information from a variety of sources. Keep a record of the behaviors you observe, including time of day and food eaten prior to a reaction. You observe behaviors and communicate them to the doctor. The doctor can help with a diagnosis.

Know that the medical community is limited to the information that you give them.

As you work with the medical professionals, listen to that little voice inside you. I urge you to trust it. When anyone suggests something for your child that makes you cringe inside, it's not right yet. Keep looking for another solution. That inner voice doesn't always interpret correctly, but it is always right when something else needs to be done. It seems we had that intuition as children, but we somehow talk ourselves out of it as adults and don't know how to interpret it any longer.

By contrast, when you have found the right solution, your inner voice will be at peace. It may be terribly hard; you may wish with all your heart that you didn't need the help—but you will know deep inside that it's the right thing to do now.

Check out the following medical community Web sites:

www.aacap.org/index.ww
www.amenclinics.com
www.nidcd.nih.gov/health/hearing
www.asha.org/public/speech/development/child_hear_talk.htm
www.brailleinstitute.org
www.irlen.com
www.oep.org

Community Agencies

You'll find a number of resources to assist you and your children in learning throughout your community. Most colleges and universities offer special reading clinics for children. Often these reading clinics are a laboratory for those preparing for a future as a teacher, so your child will help a future teacher do a better job in helping children. It's a win-win. It's also an inexpensive solution.

Call your local library, college, university, or senior center to see if they have tutorials. Check with your local churches.

Many large churches have afterschool tutorials available free. If you don't mind the bits of religious training that may accompany the tutoring, they're an excellent and free source of support for you.

There are many professional companies that offer afterschool tutoring. They range in price from free to very expensive. If you're looking for a service like that, or even a private tutor, shop around and visit each center to see if it has the "feeling tone" that you want for your child. Once again, listen to that little voice inside to decide whether or not it's right for you.

Public Libraries

Librarians are delighted when you take advantage of what they have to offer, and they have a wealth of resources. Have your children do their homework at the library where resources are readily available—from books, from the Internet, and from the librarian. Most libraries now offer online help. The Los Angeles public library, for example, has a special homework Web site. Go to *www.lapl.org/kidspath* and click on the link at the bottom of the page that says "Homework Help."

Most libraries have a community directory, available at the reference desk, that leads you to all the support services offered in the local area. Take advantage of that.

The Psychological Community

Jeff was only 2½ when his brother died and his father left. I tried to talk about it, and he would do something humorous. I thought he was too young to understand what was going on.

I was referred to Children's Hospital where they had an intern doing "play therapy." He played with Jeff while I observed behind a one-way window. What "ah-ha" moments those observations brought me!

Even at that young age, Jeff had learned to hide his emotions. When the therapist said something about his brother or his dad, Jeff would hesitate for a fraction of a second. Then he would change the subject or act the clown.

If your child is struggling to learn, he feels stupid. You may need the help of a trained therapist or trained psychologist to help you through that emotional period in your child's life.

If you have had a recent trauma in your home, your child may be grieving. Grief affects learning.

If you live with abuse or dysfunction of any kind, it will affect your child's school work.

In short, anything that hurts the heart of a child will affect school work. The psychological community is the right place to begin. They may refer you to twelve-step programs, to family counseling, to grief recovery programs, or to another support network that will help you function better as a family. The indirect result is that school work will improve when family relationships do.

 Anything that hurts the heart of a child will affect school work.

There are interns in almost every psychological clinic who work with children for a lower fee. They are graduate students serving under the supervision of a psychologist or social worker; part of their internship requires that they work under supervision for a period of time. Children's hospitals, regular hospitals, hospital chaplains, and large churches may have child and family support.

Most centers accept insurance, and most have a sliding fee structure.

Check out the following community agency Web sites:

http://2excel.net
www.alcoholics-anonymous.org
www.12step.org
www.christianrecovery.org

The Internet

The Internet is a growing field for tutoring. Online tutoring is becoming available in every subject area. Because it is so rapidly changing, to give you a list would be futile at this moment. When you need help with tutoring, use a search engine and type in key words and phrases such as *tutoring, tutoring in math, tutoring in reading, tutoring in science, my child needs help in math*—any number of key words will bring you a list of the resources available to you.

My caution to you here is the caution I would give to anyone for any subject on the Internet: check it out. Ask for credentials. Ask for references. Ask for the ability to contact someone who has received the services of the company. Ask how they are aligned with your school's curriculum and your state's academic standards. Internet resources include charlatans after an easy source of money, "tutors" who know nothing about teaching or tutoring, experts who know content but do not know how to teach, trained or professional tutors, and professional teachers.

One good way to test whether an Internet option is working or not is to try it for a little while, and watch your child. See how she responds to it. If grades improve as a result, continue the tutoring. If they don't, it is not right for you. Look for something else.

Online tutoring services range from free, to fee, to subscription. You need to check out the budget when you seek the Internet for help, as you would with anything else.

One Last Thing

You're an intelligent person. Do you really believe that prayer makes a difference?

Usually this question comes not from those making fun of me, but from those desperately seeking help for their children and begging for a source of strength and hope.

Yes, I believe in prayer. *Even if* I'm wrong, prayer helps. If it does nothing else, it helps us face honestly the facts of our dilemma and focus on finding a solution. It gathers our thought resources, generates creative ideas, and garners support through the power of positive thinking. A friend said it this way:

I know you believe in prayer. I don't know what I believe, but when things were tough this year, I tried it. It helped.

Begin with the End in Mind

When I read Habit Two in the *7 Habits of Highly Effective People,* Covey told us to remove distractions and plan to spend some time on this chapter, because it would change our lives. I thought, "How pompous! I have read a dozen books on goal-setting, and none of them have changed my life."

After I read the chapter, I had to agree with Covey. I made some personal changes in my life as a result of reading his book. I read it in the aftermath of a time of personal trauma. I was grieving over the loss of a son and the loss of a marriage. What changed me so dramatically was when he had us attend our own funeral and envision what our children would say.

What I wanted Jeff to say about living with me was: "Living with Mom was so much fun. We had a blast together."

Had Jeff been honest at the time I read the book, he would have said, "All she does is sit around the house and cry."

I made lifelong changes as a result of reading that book. I did learn to "begin with the end in mind" and to create in Jeff the values and the relationships that I want him to remember and that I hope will mold his life.

I have to ask you those questions now:

What is important to you?

What values do you want to pass on to your children?

How do you want to be remembered?

What do you want them to be like as adults?

Even in the issue of homework, remember to keep your personal values and beliefs at the forefront. Remember, this is a long-term assignment. Sometimes you will lose a battle in order to win a war. And, of course, your personal relationship with your children is far more important than whether or not they complete the homework assignment.

···················· REFLECTION ···················

In my business, we hear often about how "overprotective" Hispanic fathers are of their little girls. We're told they won't allow their daughters to spend the night away from home.

I sat in the living room of the Hispanic parents' homes, the African American parents' homes, and all my other parents' homes promising to care for their sons and daughters if they could accompany me on a week-long field trip.

They all were allowed to go.

By the way, this little white mamma wouldn't allow her son to spend the night in the home of someone I didn't know. It's really just good parenting. It is the language of love.

Appendix A

Learning Theories

1. If you say and/or write a fact over and over again, you will put it in your memory very firmly.
2. When memorizing facts, material becomes rote after the third repetition. Therefore, rotate material to be memorized in sets of three repetitions.
3. Optimum time for memorization is five to fifteen minutes at intervals of two to twenty-four hours.
4. The more senses that are involved in the learning process, the more rapidly learning will occur.
5. Study a few items at a time.
6. Study only what you don't know.
7. When students know what to expect, they are likely to adjust their behavior to receive the reward and avoid problems.
8. If you ask yourself a question to which the new information is the right answer, then say the fact to yourself as the answer, you will increase your memory capability.
9. It is easier to remember information if it is associated with something you already know.
10. If you set up categories before beginning to read, it is easier to notice things that fit into the categories, thus easier to remember.
11. It is easier to remember new information if you make an absurd association.
12. If material is personalized, it is remembered longer.

13. A student will learn material more thoroughly if asked to explain it to someone else.
14. It is best to schedule your studying so you don't study like subjects in sequence.
15. Students will tend to study more effectively and avoid burnout if they build refreshing and rewarding breaks into their study period.

Appendix B

Common Terms and Strategies

Aha: Something new to you, or a new twist to something that you haven't thought about before, or something poignant that was reinforced in the lesson. An ah-ha needs to be stated in one sentence or less. This is often used to review or to help verbalize learning when the student suddenly understands.

Group Norms: Guidelines that everyone in the class agrees to before you begin an activity. Sample group norms include: everyone's viewpoint will be respected; no one will be laughed at; no idea will be ignored; when one person is talking, everyone will listen; what's said here stays here; etc.

Role Play: Acting out a situation. It allows students to think and feel from another person's perspective (e.g., walk a mile in another person's moccasins).

Splash Down: A technique where students free-write for one to three minutes whatever comes into their mind. Students, when they are angry or troubled about something, splash their worries down on paper so their minds can focus on material to be learned. These writings are usually private. If your children choose to share it with you, value it and talk to them about it.

Think-Pair-Share: A strategy where a student thinks about a response to a question, then finds one other person with whom to share his thinking.

Think-Pair-Share-Square: A variation of Think-Pair-Share. In this process, an individual student in the think process focuses on two to three important items. Two students then "pair and share." Together, they synthesize, or condense, them into what they both believe to be the three most important items. Then they join two other students to form a "square." In the square process, each team of two would pair with another team of two to create a square. Within the square, they would compare their answers and then come up with the important items that all four of them agree on.

Three-Minute Quick Write: Students are allowed three minutes to write everything that comes to their mind about a given topic as fast as they can. This is used to help students refocus and synthesize at the end of a lesson or to help students focus on and personalize material at the beginning of the lesson. These are usually not collected, but may be turned in as a part of their notebook or journal.

Venn Diagram: A Venn diagram consists of two overlapping circles. It's used to compare likes and differences. Where the circles overlap, in the middle, you put "likes," and on either side, you would put "differences" from each of two separate sources. For example, you might have students interview their parents and create a Venn diagram. In the middle would be those areas where parents and students agree. On the left would be student viewpoints, and on the right would be parent viewpoints.

Whip: You "whip around the room" with each person, or group, making a one-sentence statement about the topic. This is often used for closure in a lesson to help reinforce key points and for reporting out after a cooperative learning activity.

Appendix C

The 12 Brain-Based Principles of Learning

1. All learning engages the physiology.
2. The brain/mind is social.
3. The search for meaning is innate.
4. The search for meaning occurs through patterning.
5. Emotions are critical to patterning.
6. The brain/mind processes parts and wholes simultaneously.
7. Learning involves both focused attention and peripheral perception.
8. Learning is both conscious and unconscious.
9. There are at least two approaches to memory.
10. Learning is developmental.
11. Complex learning is enhanced by challenge and inhibited by threat associated with helplessness and fatigue.
12. Each brain is uniquely organized.

Bibliography

Amen, Daniel G., MD. *Making a Good Brain Great* (New York: Harmony Books, 2005).

Amen, Daniel G., MD. *The Secrets of Successful Students* (Fairfield, California: MindWorks Press, 2005).

American Academy of Child and Adolescent Psychiatry. "Teens: Alcohol and Other Drugs." Available at *http://aacap.org/page.ww?section=Facts+for+Families&name=Teens%3A+Alcohol+And+Other+Drugs*.

American Academy of Child and Adolescent Psychiatry. *Facts for Families*, "The Depressed Child," 2006, www.aacap.org.

American Speech, Language, and Hearing Association, *www.asha.org/public/speech/development/child_hear_talk.htm*.

Armstrong, Thomas. *Multiple Intelligences in the Classroom* (Association for Supervision and Curriculum Development: Alexandria, Virginia, 1994).

Blanchard, Ken. *Leadership and the One Minute Manager: Increasing Effectiveness Through Situational Leadership* (New York: William Morrow and Company, Inc., 1999).

Bloom, Benjamin S. "An Introduction to Mastery Learning Theory," in *Schools, Society, and Mastery Learning*, ed. J. H. Block (New York: Holt, Rinehart and Winston, 1974).

Brandt, Millicent Hume. "Improving Auditory Sequencing Skills in the Kindergarten-Age Child through the Increased Instruction of Music" (ED324132) (dissertation/thesis–practicum paper, 1986). Available at *www.eric.ed.gov*.

Caine, Renate Nummela, Geoffrey Caine, Carol Lynn McClintic, and Karl J. Klimek. *12 Brain/Mind Learning Principles in Action: The Fieldbook for Making Connections, Teaching, and the Human Brain* (Thousand Oaks, California: Corwin Press, 2004).

Caine, Geoffrey, Renate Nummela Caine, and Sam Crowell. *Mind-Shifts* (Tucson, Arizona: Zephyr Press, 1994).

Colbert, Ty, PhD. *Achieving Competitive Excellence* (Santa Ana, California: Kevco Publishing, 1996).

Colbert, Ty, PhD. *Broken Brains or Wounded Hearts* (Santa Ana, California: Kevco Publishing, 1996).

Covey, Stephen R. *The 7 Habits of Highly Effective People* (New York: Free Press, 1990).

Dobson, James. *The New Hide or Seek: Building Self-Esteem in Your Child* (Grand Rapids, Michigan: Revell, 1999).

Gardner, Howard. *Frames of Mind: The Theory of Multiple Intelligences* (New York: Basic Books, 1993).

Glasser, William. *The Quality School* (New York: Harper Paperbacks, 1998).

Glasser, William. *Schools Without Failure* (New York: Harper and Row, 1975).

Golay, Dr. Keith. *Learning Patterns & Temperament Styles* (Fullerton, California: Manas Systems, 1982).

Hodgkinson, Harold. *All One System: A Second Look* (Institute for Educational Leadership: Washington, DC, 1999).

Irlen, Helen. *Reading by the Colors*, rev. ed. (New York: Perigee Books, 2005).

Johnson, David & Roger and Edythe Holubec. *Circles of Learning*, 5th ed. (Edina, Minnesota: Interaction Book Company, 2002).

Kagan, Spencer, Dr. *Cooperative Learning* (San Clemente, California: Kagan Cooperative Learning, 1994).

Keirsey, David. *Please Understand Me II: Temperament, Character, Intelligence* (Del Mar, California: Prometheus Nemesis Book Company, 1998).

Linksman, Ricki, MEd. "The Fine Line Between ADHD and Kinesthetic Learners," Reprinted from *Latitudes*, vol. 1, no. 6, 2006, Association for Comprehensive NeuroTherapy. Available at *www.latitudes.org/articles/learn01.html*.

Littauer, Florence. *Personality Plus* (Tarrytown, NY: Revell, 1992).

Littauer, Florence. *Your Personality Tree* (Nashville, TN: W Publishing Group, 2005).

Lockett, Sharon Marshall. *Smarter, Not Harder!* (Laguna Niguel, California: CLASS Services, Educational Innovations, 1998; 2005), *www.score-ed.com*.

Lockett, Sharon Marshall. *SCORE Staff Development Guide* (Laguna Niguel, California: Educational Innovations, 2006), *www.score-ed.com*.

Lockett, Sharon Marshall. *Study Skills for Student Success* (Laguna Niguel, California: Educational Innovations, 2006), *www.score-ed.com*.

Lockett, Sharon Marshall, *Crisis, Grief, and Loss . . . and How to Help Your Students Through It* (Laguna Niguel, California: Educational Innovations/SCORE, 2001), *www.score-ed.com*.

Mann, Raymond E. "The Effect of Music and Sound Effects on Listening Comprehension of Fourth Grade Students" (ED172738) (speech/meeting paper; report—research, 1979). Available at *www.eric.ed.gov*.

Marshall, Sharon and Jeff Johnson. *Take My Hand: Guiding your Child Through Grief* (Grand Rapids, Michigan: Zondervan, 2001).

Marshall, Sharon. *Justin, Heaven's Baby* (Laguna Niguel, California: Educational Innovations, 2002).

Jason Millman and Walter Pauk. *How to Take Tests* (New York: McGraw-Hill Book Co., 1969).

National Institute on Deafness and Other Communication Disorders, National Institutes of Health, *www.nidcd.nih.gov/health/hearing*.

Optometric Extension Program Foundation, Inc. 1921 E. Carnegie Ave., Ste 3L

Santa Ana, CA 92705 *Does Your Child Have a Learning-Related Vision Problem?* Pamphlet. Available at *www.oep.org/Patients&ParentsHome.asp.*

Princeton Review, *11 Practice Tests for the New SAT and PSAT* (Princeton Review, 2005).

Rauscher, Frances, PhD. "The Mozart Effect." *www.uwosh.edu/psychology/rauscher.htm*

Robinson, F. P. *Effective Study*, 4th ed. (New York: HarperCollins, 1970).

Scott, Fannie, *100 Years of Memories!*, compiled and self-published by her seven children in honor of her 100th birthday, July 19, 1991.

Sternberg, Robert J. *Wisdom, Intelligence, and Creativity Synthesized, (New York; Cambridge University Press, 2003); www.yale.edu/rjsternberg*

Treisman, Uri, *Teaching Growth and Effectiveness: An Issues Paper.* 1994; *www.utdanacenter.org.*

Treisman, Philip Uri and Stephanie A. Surles. "Systemic reform and minority student high achievement." In *The Right Thing to Do, the Smart Thing to Do: Enhancing Diversity in the Health Professions in Honor of Herbert W. Nickens, MD*, pp. 260–280. (Washington, DC: Institute of Medicine, National Academies Press, 2001). Available at *http://newton.nap.edu/books/0309076145/html/260.html.*

United States Department of Education. *Helping Your Child with Homework*, rev. 2005. Pamphlet. Available at *http://www.ed.gov/parents/academic/help/homework/index.html.*

Index